Beachcombing and Beachcraft

Joyce Pope

illustrated by Patricia Mynott and
The Tudor Art Agency Limited

TREASURE PRESS

FOREWORD

The seashore is an ever-changing environment. Land becomes sea when the tide rolls in and sea becomes land when the tide ebbs. This constant change is only part of the fascination of the seashore for each wave is a continuously varying individual, with its own diversifications on the general pattern of advance and retreat. The effects of sunlight and shade on the breaking water can enhance still further the enjoyment a visitor can derive from his surroundings. Changes to the beach itself are brought about by the power of the sea, which also sweeps ashore both living and man-made things and, in many instances, removes them again. Many objects of use and beauty are brought in briefly by the waves, forming a temporary and constantly changing part of the beach scene which is the main source of interest to the beachcomber. This book attempts to describe the main types of booty to be discovered on the shore and suggests uses for some of them. A holiday, or a lifetime, can sometimes be enriched by beachcombing, an activity which can be indulged in with any degree of energy or lethargy for any length of time that is desired – an intrinsic variation which can only add to its pleasure.

J.P.

The illustration on page 11 is reproduced from a Geological Survey Map with the permission of the Controller, H.M.S.O. Crown copyright reserved.

First published in Great Britain in 1975 by The Hamlyn Publishing Group Limited

This edition published in Great Britain in 1989 by
Treasure Press
Michelin House
81 Fulham Road
London SW3 6RB

ISBN 1 85051 427 5

Printed in Yugoslavia by Mladinska Knjiga.

CONTENTS

THE BEACH

Beaches are found where land and sea meet and may be defined as the zone at the edge of the land which is covered daily by the tide. Conditions found there are unique, and the plants and animals found there occur nowhere else and could not survive on dry land nor in the open oceans. Below tide level is the open sea, which is a region of stability, varying only slightly in temperature, salinity, acidity and the other parameters of life. Above the tide line lies the dry land which varies greatly in temperature from day to night and from season to season, but where desiccation demands that at least the larger plants and animals maintain their own exact balance of liquids and salts, encapsulated in waterproof skins.

The beach is a place of abrupt variety. As the tide rolls out, the exposed area dries in the sun and wind and the temperature of the surface, or of shallow pools, may become very high, only to be lowered suddenly when the rising tide brings cool water splashing back again. Drying out is a danger for organisms of the upper part of the beach, but most are pro-

The beach, washed twice daily by the tides, may be rocky, pebbly or sandy, but holiday-makers are found on all types.

tected by thick shells or by the habit of burrowing into moist places while the tide is low, although creatures well adapted against dryness may be in danger of drowning once the water returns. In pools near the top of the beach the water evaporates on a warm day, increasing the salinity, although if the weather is wet, salt levels will be reduced to far below those of the open sea. Few organisms, except those of the beach, could stand such variations. The beach is also a place of violent activity for here the forces of wind and water find their way barred, and waves which have free motion at sea break, crashing hundreds of tons of water on to the obstructing land. They tear boulders from the cliffs and smash them into pebbles, which are eventually ground into sand.

On the beach, then, we may often find the dead but still decorative remains of shells and other animals or plants as well as debris, lost or abandoned at sea, which litters the strandline and which is the basic material of the beachcomber's interest.

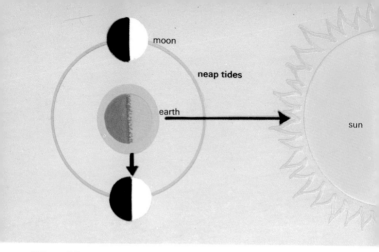

The tides

Twice each day the sea encroaches towards the land and is dragged back on itself again. These movements are known as the tides and are mainly the result of the interaction between the gravitational forces of a rotating moon circulating the rotating earth. They are able to move large bodies of liquid, such as the water in the ocean basins, although they can scarcely be detected on land. The pull of the moon attracts the water facing it causing a bulge, and consequently a high tide. On the other side of the earth there is a similar bulge of water resulting from the moon attracting the earth towards itself more than it attracts the water on that side; thus the water is left behind. As the earth completes a single turn on its axis in slightly less than twenty-four hours, the two waves – each of which causes a high tide – are separated from each other by about eleven hours and thirty-five minutes and so the time of the tide shifts each day.

A complicating factor is that the world's oceans are broken into a series of basins by the great land masses and, although there is some spill from one basin to the next, each tends to behave as a separate entity, in which there is an oscillation of the water on a roughly twelve hour period. In most places on the coast the height of the tides varies considerably. On some occasions water may be pushed back by high winds, or affected by local conditions such as may be found in a long, narrow

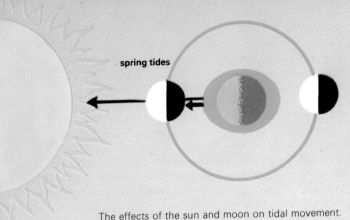

spring tides

The effects of the sun and moon on tidal movement.

bay. The major factor influencing the tide height, however, is the sun which although so much further away than the moon also exerts a detectable gravitational pull on the earth. The final effect of this is variable, for at different times of the month the sun and moon are in different positions relative to each other and to the earth. At periods of new and full moon these are such that they augment each other's efforts and the tidal movements are then at their greatest. These are called *spring tides,* at whatever time of year they may occur. At periods of half moon the sun and moon are pulling at right angles to each other, cancelling out each other's force, and the effect is that there is less tidal movement. These are referred to as *neap tides.*

The time of the tide varies at different points along the coast as the tidal wave arrives. The main tidal wave which travels west to east across the Atlantic strikes the south-west coast of Ireland and is divided, part being diverted up the west coast and part being pushed along the south Irish coast and towards the English Channel. Here the narrowing funnel shape forces the water to behave as if it were in a separate basin, with a null point in the region of Portland Bill. This largely accounts for the complex tidal patterns and currents of the area, especially where the flow is broken by headlands and promontories.

Longshore drift

Beneath the shore sloping down from the land is a shelving platform cut by the waves, and the sand and gravel resting on this may be moved each time the tide is high. In some cases it may be a straightforward up and down movement, but beach material is often carried along the coast and in many places breakwaters are built in an attempt to delay this process. Where this is done it is usually possible to see the direction of movement for on one side of the groyne the level of the beach is much higher than on the other, where the sand has been scoured away. This lateral movement is called *longshore drift* and is explained by the fact that waves rarely strike the beach entirely parallel to the land. As they run up the beach they may carry sand or pebbles, but once their force is spent they return to the sea by the shortest route dragging some of the pebbles with them, which they often displace by a distance of several metres. There is also drift below the tide line, often caused by the 'parachute' effect of large seaweeds which float on the water and pull the stones to which they are attached along the shoreline.

The effects of groynes on longshore drift.

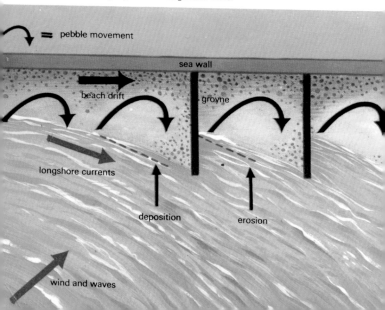

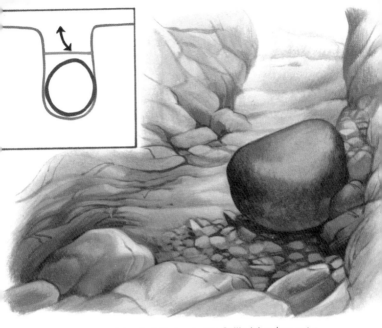

This boulder on the island of Bryher in the Scilly Isles, has cut a notch in the cliffs and is rolled up and down with the rise and fall of the tides.

Many beaches show a gradation of material from the land to the sea, with the largest stones or pebbles at the top of the beach and fine sand towards low water mark. This is because the waves travelling up the beach have the greatest force and power to carry objects, but as they return they have little energy and stones dropped at the top of the beach cannot be carried back again. If the slope is steep some may roll down, but in general the biggest boulders lie high up the shore. These will probably have been hurled there during storms, which are the periods of greatest change on the beach. In some places a single storm has been known to sweep the entire beach away, leaving only the rocky platform below, and in other places huge mounds of beach material have been brought and deposited far above the usual reach of the sea. It is after storms that we can see cliff falls and other major changes in the shape of the beach.

BEACH FORM AND GEOLOGY

Geology is one of the most important influences determining the exact shape and form of any beach. Where outcrops of hard rocks occur, they generally form cliffs and headlands; where the rocks are soft, bays and beaches are to be found.

This may be seen in a broad sense in Britain, by comparing the east coast, from Essex to Norfolk, with the coast of Devon and Cornwall. The former is backed by soft rocks, and has sandy or pebbly beaches, with only low cliffs which in many places are being rapidly worn away. The latter, which is an area of old, hard rocks, has steep cliffs broken by small bays and erosion is taking place more slowly. In some places a small outcrop of hard rock may change a section of the beach, as for example at Bognor Regis on the south coast of England, where an outcrop of hard stone, called the Bognor Rocks, makes a series of boulders and rock pools running down the beach. These hard rocks are surrounded by the soft and easily eroded London Clay, which makes a level beach with no pools or boulders.

The softer rocks on land are more easily eroded than the hard ones and rivers are often found where a band of clay separates harder rocks such as sandstones. This principle affects the form of many shorelines where we often find that a bay is horseshoe shaped. The land behind the middle of the bay is low lying and made of softer or weaker rocks and here a river will have carved a valley. The arms of the bay are often cliffed, forming headlands which represent the continuation of the ridges which bounded the valley. In a bay of this kind there will be considerable variation of the beach sediments, the finest sand being where the stream brings silt down to the sea and coarser sand occurring towards the outer edges of the bay.

The seashore may show more obvious results of earth movements, for here we can often see raised beaches which represent a period, now long past, when the sea level stood higher than it does at the present. In other areas there may be evidence of times when it was lower, usually in the form of submerged forests which are uncovered at low tide.

This geological map demonstrates how hard rocks form headlands and soft rocks become eroded to form bays.

TOR

BAY

PAIGNTON

BRIXHAM

BERRY

Churston
Ferrers

	alluvium (silt)		limestone		slates
	river gravels		slates and shales		igneous rocks
	conglomerate and sandstone		sandstones and shales		
	slates and mudstone				

11

Rock and boulder beaches

The old, hard rocks of western and northern Britain often form cliffs where they meet the sea. In such places there may be no beach at all and the water beats against a rock wall, fretting it into caves at various points of weakness. Even in the summer time there may be storms when the sea beats more than thirty metres up the steep rock face. An indication of how high the water reaches may be obtained by noting the lowest level at which the cliff-nesting kittiwakes build their nests, for although they may tolerate occasional spray they cannot stand the full force of the waves and must site their nurseries above all danger of destruction. The full power of the waves is reached in the storms of winter when, armed with stones they have picked up from the beach, they batter at the cliffs, tearing and destroying them.

The result of this activity may be the formation of boulder beaches, such as those at the northern end of the Cliffs of Moher in County Clare, Ireland. The waves which tear at these cliffs are whipped up by a wind which has had no obstruction as it travels from America. The boulders at the base of the cliff range in size up to about ten metres in diameter. Few organisms can survive in such a place, for the sea pounds and smashes everything against the cliff. Sometimes in such places, erosion has broken the cliffs down to a series of rocky coves with small bays, and here life can flourish. There will be shelter from the wind and waves – from some directions at least – and the rock offers a firm foothold to the sedentary plants and animals of the beach. This gives us the richest of all the seashore environments, with a very large number of species of plants and animals.

Beachcombing in a place such as the Cliffs of Moher is likely to be difficult and dangerous. Anything swept ashore will probably be destroyed and even reaching the beach may present difficulties. It is on the gentler shores of lower cliffs with little, sandy coves that beachcombing of all sorts is at its best, whether one is looking for living things or the wreck of the sea cast gently ashore.

The wave-battered boulder beach and Cliffs of Moher in County Clare, Ireland.

Pebble beaches

Pebble beaches are to be found in many places round the coast, particularly in low-lying areas, where longshore drift may bring stones from a considerable distance. A pebble beach is a place of constant change, for every high tide alters it slightly while major storms can not only change the profile of a beach but can also remove a large section of it entirely. They frequently form spits or long, narrow promontories, often running parallel to the shore, as at Orford Ness in England, where the river Alde is prevented from reaching the open sea for nearly eighteen kilometres by the great mound of shingle which deflects its course southwards.

Where a spit ends the swirling sea currents often cause a landward bend to be formed, giving a hook-shaped appearance to the spit as a whole, but as it grows such hooks are left behind, although on large shingle beaches they may remain as ridges running at an angle to the line of the main beach, giving us evidence of the growth of the area as a whole.

The profile of a pebble beach usually shows a series of ridges parallel with the sea. These represent the levels to which

Millions of pebbles, transported by the sea, grind each other to flattened, oval shapes on shingle beaches.

storms or extra high tides have thrown the stones and as with boulder beaches we often find that the largest stones lie on the uppermost ridges where the force of the waves has hurled them. In spite of the gradation in size of stone from the upper to the lower beach, there is seldom any marked size in grading along it. An exception can be seen at Chesil Beach, England, where the stones vary from the size of a clenched fist at one end to that of a sparrow's egg at the other.

The constant movement of pebbles on a shingle beach makes it an extremely inhospitable place for living things and shingle ridges form the most barren of all types of beach. The power of the sea grinds the pebbles against each other eventually wearing them into a flattened, oval shape however hard the type of rock of which they were formed. No organism, however well protected, can stand the strength of these millstones. Besides this, the pebbles are too large to carry a constant film of moisture and their dryness deprives even the hardiest plant or animal of the chance of survival. For the beachcomber, the pebbles may themselves be rewarding but it is rare to find other treasure here.

Sandy beaches and dunes

Pebbles are eventually ground down to sand and these almost irreducible fragments, often of quartz, form some of the most attractive holiday beaches. They often slope down very gently to the sea and huge areas dry out at low tide when the water may retreat for a kilometre or more.

At first sight a sandy beach may appear to be completely devoid of life, for there are few surface-dwelling organisms here, but the multitude of worm castings and small depressions in the beach shows that this is not so and hidden beneath the surface is a teeming, dark world of living things. Except for the uppermost part of the beach, which may dry out completely, each sand grain is wrapped in a jacket of water which supports a huge abundance and variety of microscopic animals. Protozoans and minute worms are important in these populations and larger animals, such as lugworms and cockles, lie protected beneath the sand reaching to the surface at high tide to feed on microscopic organisms brought to them by the sea. These animals may live in incredibly dense populations – one small bivalve has been recorded at over 1,000 per square metre.

Sandy beaches provide the material for dunes, which grow and shift on their landward edge, but become stabilized with plant growth.

At low tide, as the surface sand dries, it is blown by the wind, often forming an area of dunes at the back of the beach. These may start to grow round any obstruction, but constantly change shape until they are stabilized by the growth of specialized plants, such as marram grass. Dunes are of great interest to naturalists, as the plants and animals found there may occur nowhere else, but the conservation of the habitat is often difficult for a break in the fragile plant cover may result in a 'blow out' and widespread destruction of the environment.

Mud and silt, which have an even finer grain structure than sand, may accumulate in some protected areas, forming salt marshes and becoming stabilized by rooted plants. Although these are very different from the seaweeds of the open shore they, too, are adapted to withstand the daily incursions of the sea.

For the beachcomber, sandy beaches offer the best opportunity to hunt for real treasure – coins and valuables dropped by visitors to these areas. Cargoes and other objects swept ashore from the sea suffer less damage than on rocky beaches, and sand and mudflats are often the best places for exciting and even valuable finds.

Fossils

Fossils form one of the types of treasure to be found on many beaches and although these relics of the distant past may have little or no intrinsic monetary worth, the excitement of finding a good specimen is as rewarding to many people as the discovery of more valuable objects.

Most fossils were formed when the remains of dead plants or animals were buried in the silt of rivers, or on the seabed. Although the soft parts such as skin or muscle are almost always totally destroyed, the hard parts such as shells or teeth may be preserved as the silt hardens into rock, and when this is eroded away the fossils may be uncovered. The battering of the sea against the shore often exposes fossils, which may then be found on the beach. Usually they are the remains of small invertebrate animals which lie mixed with the shells of recently dead sea creatures, not easily distinguished from them. An example of this may be seen on the south coast of

Mary Anning made a living by selling fossils to Victorian collectors.

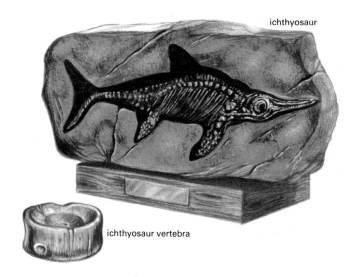

ichthyosaur

ichthyosaur vertebra

Complete skeletons of ichthyosaurs, with the soft parts intact, have only been found in Germany.

England, near to Chichester, where turret shells and a form of large cockle eroded from the Bracklesham Beds lie on the sand. These were alive about fifty million years ago, but are so similar to their modern relatives that they often go unnoticed. Forms more dramatically different from modern animals may be discovered in older rocks, such as the Liassic exposures of the Lyme Regis area on the south coast of England. Here the fossils are the remains of animals which lived about 170 million years ago and include ammonites and the swimming reptiles called ichthyosaurs and plesiosaurs as well as flying pterosaurs.

A famous fossil hunter who searched the beaches of Lyme Regis during the last century was Mary Anning. Orphaned at the age of eleven, she managed to support her brothers and sisters by collecting and selling fossils from the beach, a task in which she had previously helped her father. Her market was the tourists who, with the development of the fashion for taking the sea air, were beginning to patronize Lyme Regis. It is said that she started her career as a fossil hunter by selling an ammonite to two ladies for half a crown. Later she was to discover the first complete plesiosaur, the first ichthyosaur and the first pterosaur to be recorded in Britain. Many specimens of these animals to be seen today in out museums were collected by Mary Anning. Today, much of the cliff area near to Lyme Regis where Mary Anning used to search for fossils is shored up by concrete, so erosion is largely halted and the sea cannot uncover any more fossils. Specimens of the vertebrae of plesiosaurs or ichthyosaurs may still be picked up occasionally, however. Apart from their intrinsic interest, they have a pleasing, simple shape similar to a shallow dish. The beachcomber, who hates to waste anything, may use them as such or as paperweights.

Another place in Britain where soft rocks are eroded into cliffs by the sea is on the Isle of Sheppey in Kent. Here at Warden Point the London Clay forms cliffs about fifty metres high but each year the sea bites further into them and, especially during the winter storms, washes large amounts of clay down on to the beach. The London Clay was formed about sixty million years ago, under conditions similar to those in some parts of south-east Asia today. The plant fossils are mainly of species with tropical affinities, such as the fruits of the nipa palm and cinnamon which, at first glance, often looks like small beads. The remains of animals are abundant and include several sorts of snails and other shells, starfishes, crabs and lobsters, as well as fish (especially the teeth of sharks), a snake and several kinds of turtle, the shells of which may reach thirty centimetres in length. These turtles are rarities, however, and not likely to be found very often. Nevertheless, even the casual visitor is bound to come away from the beach with some treasures, for invertebrate fossils are very abundant in the cliffs. There is no need to look for them there, however, for the sea sorts them as it washes down the beach and small groups of objects all of the same size and weight accumulate in an area perhaps no larger than a dinner plate, and may contain as many as twenty sharks' teeth or small fossil snails all gathered together.

The result of a typical day's beachcombing for fossils. Concretions are not true fossils.

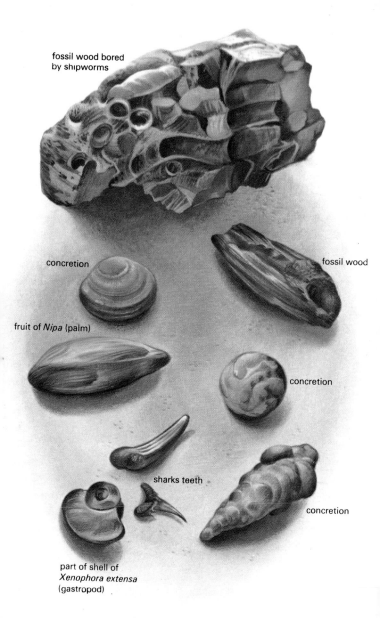

fossil wood bored
by shipworms

concretion

fossil wood

fruit of *Nipa* (palm)

concretion

sharks teeth

concretion

part of shell of
Xenophora extensa
(gastropod)

21

SEASHORE LIFE

Zonation of seashore life

Two factors, above all others, control the distribution of plants and animals on the beach. These are light and water and, since both vary with the tides which bring water but filter out light, we find that life on the shore is zoned from the upper to the lower beach. Plants of the upper region are capable of withstanding desiccation, but need strong light, while those of the lower beach are adapted to low light intensities but are unable to survive long periods out of water. Light is less important to animals but, as on land, there is a relationship between herbivores and their food plants, which accounts for part of the zonation. In general, the ability to survive drying out is found in animals living near the top of

Different plants and animals are found at varying levels on the shore.

splash zone

upper shore

the shore, while those on the lower levels die if they are out of water for long.

The zones of the beach, which are fairly clear-cut, are classified as follows. At the top of the shore is the **splash zone**. This is never fully covered by water, but is subject to the influence of salt spray. Below this is the **upper shore**, which is covered only by the waters of the high spring tides. The **middle shore**, which may be subdivided, is covered and exposed by the rise and fall of the average tide. The **lower shore** is exposed only by low spring tides. Below this is the **sub-littoral zone**, which is never uncovered, but from which some specimens may be swept up on to the beach. Each zone has certain characteristic plants and animals and although there may be some overlap, in British waters no single organism occurs throughout the whole tidal range.

middle shore   lower shore   sub-littoral zone

Studying seashore life

The pleasures of the shore are enormously increased by a knowledge of its inhabitants, which are often colourful and beautiful to look at and which with very few exceptions in temperate waters are entirely harmless to man. A good rule to start with is not to be too ambitious; few people could claim to know every plant and animal on the beach by sight, so don't be discouraged if you find difficulty in identifying any particular organism. Getting to know the major groups of animals which you are likely to meet is quite easy and once the general pattern of their structure is learnt, recognizing the different species becomes simpler.

It is a good idea to take a slow, thoughtful look at the beach. Sit quietly by the side of a rock pool for a while and wait for its inhabitants to show themselves to you. By looking at them the first step in your study has already been taken. Discovering what they are is the second step, for understanding the life of the beach must include some knowledge of what is there. A great many books have been produced which will help you to identify what you find, so it is as well to arm yourself with one of these before you visit the shore. Besides a book to help you with identification, a note book is essential. In it you can make a list of the things that you have found, where they occur on the beach and the time of day or part of the year that they appear to be active. It doesn't have to be an elaborate book – a shorthand pad with a stiff cover is ideal. Write in pencil or ball point, which won't run when it gets wet.

Identification of the creatures of the shore often requires some magnification of their features and a handlens, preferably one magnifying by ten times, is necessary. Tie it on a piece of string and hang it round your neck – lenses are among the most easily mislaid objects. You will need to catch many of the smaller animals before you can look at them closely. For this you will need nets; one with a one centimetre mesh for shrimps, prawns etc., and one with a mesh of not more than one millimetre for smaller creatures. For work in rock pools and shallow water it is better to use a net with a short handle, rather than one which is too long and can get in the way. Your catch can best be examined in a shallow tray – an old enamel baking dish is ideal – and kept, if need be, in jars which you must remember to shade from the bright sun, which most beach creatures shun if they can.

An observation aquarium

Strange as it may seem there are many details of the life histories and behaviour of even our common seashore organisms which remain to be discovered and amateurs may easily make observations which have not been recorded before. In general it is best to make any investigation of the animals in their natural environment but, for simple behavioural studies such as food preferences or reaction to light intensities or for close-up photography, it may be necessary to keep the creatures in an aquarium for a short

Some useful equipment for studying seashore life.

polythene bags

penknife

long-handled net

jars

short-handled net

enamel tray

time. Marine aquaria can be maintained for long periods and there are many books in which excellent descriptions of how to do this are given. We are not concerned here with keeping plants and animals on a long-term basis but rather maintaining them for a short time, to enable us to discover just what they are, to make simple observations or to photograph them.

For this, small, lightweight plastic tanks, which can be bought quite cheaply, are adequate. Before putting any animals into them they should be prepared by placing a layer of sand or fine gravel about five centimetres thick over the bottom, then filled with sea water and allowed to stand for a while to let any silt settle. A large stone or some pebbles will give shelter, but do not put seaweeds in as they cannot re-attach themselves and will only die and foul the water. If you wish to keep the animals for more than a day or so you will need to use an aerator. For a short time you can manage without one, however, and by not overstocking and keeping the tank as cool and shaded as possible, your animals should not suffer. It is as well to restrict the kinds of animals in any one tank. Shrimps would not survive long in the company of sea anemones, and small crabs or fishes might prove a meal for others of their own kind. Sea anemones are easy and un-demanding to keep and watch for a short time, as are gastropod molluscs, although many of these, such as top shells or periwinkles, are very active and you will need to devise a gauze cover for your tank to keep them in. Sea hares may be kept for a time but are best in a tank on their own, for their defensive ink is liable to be harmful to other creatures except in very low concentrations. Any animals which need to filter large quantities of water to get food or oxygen are least likely to do well; sea squirts and bivalve molluscs should be kept for the shortest possible time unless you intend to set up a more elaborate aquarium.

When you have finished observing the animals, return them to the beach as near as possible to the place where you found them. In the past the damage done by naturalists collecting and destroying seashore life has been considerable, and now that we realize this it is up to us not to continue a bad tradition.

Some of the animals that you can catch and watch in a small aquarium.

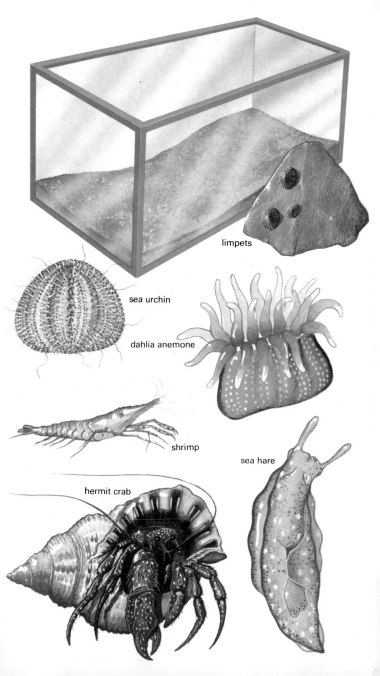

limpets

sea urchin

dahlia anemone

shrimp

sea hare

hermit crab

Rooted plants and lichens of the seashore

Although no seaweed can live in completely dry places, a number of land plants have invaded the edge of the shore. In places sheltered from the forces of waves and currents, salt marshes may form supporting dense communities of flowering plants which are capable of withstanding total submersion at least during the time of high spring tides.

On the lower levels of muddy or sandy shores eel grass (*Zostera*) is sometimes found. This holds its own by means of creeping roots and its long, narrow, green leaves certainly look grass-like. The flowers are inconspicuous and unusual in that the sea performs the task of pollination, carrying pollen from one blossom to another. Glasswort is another plant with inconspicuous flowers. It may be found in the lower parts of salt marshes, its bright-green, succulent stems standing stiffly above the zone of uncolonized mud. Townsend's cord grass is unusual in that it is a natural hybrid between a British and an American species, and was first recorded in Southampton Water, England, in 1870. More robust than either of its parents, it is now a dominant plant in many salt marshes, trapping silt and causing rapid build up of the marsh. Sea purslane is often to be seen on the slopes of channels in a salt marsh and is rarely submerged by the tide for long. The beautiful sea lavender occurs at higher levels still, as does thrift which may also be found where conditions are suitable within the splash zone of a rocky shore.

Zonation of yellow and black lichens in the splash zone.

Xanthoria parietina

Lichina pygmaea

sea lavender   sea aster   glasswort

Some rooted plants of the muddy shore.

In the upper parts of sandy beaches and on dunes, the yellow horned poppy lives up to its name when, after flowering, the seed pods develop into fantastic, long horns. The handsome, blue-green sea holly also lives in sandy places, but is all too often destroyed by picking or uprooting. On shingle banks sea campion and sea pea make a precarious living among the shifting stones. Sea pea has roots which may anchor it over twelve metres deep, but unlike most plants it cannot tolerate humus and its seeds always colonize fresh shingle. A plant which is found in many maritime habitats, but never actually grows on the seashore itself, is the scurvy grass which is not, in fact, a grass but a member of the wallflower family. It is so called because the fleshy leaves were collected by sailors for their anti-scorbutic properties.

In the splash zone of a rocky shore, lichens often occur. The green tufts of *Ramelina* grow furthest from the sea, but at about high water level two distinct lines may be seen; the upper a narrow, golden band of *Xanthoria* and below this a broader, black zone of *Verrucaria,* its encrusting granules tar-like in their appearance.

29

Green algae

Large marine algae, or seaweeds, are the most obvious plants on the majority of shores. Flaccid and slippery at low tide they are unattractive objects, but when supported by the water they are often extremely beautiful. They are fundamentally different from land plants in that they have no roots but are attached to rocks or breakwaters by holdfasts, the shape of which may be very variable. They absorb all the nutrients that they need directly from sea water and although they reproduce in a variety of ways, it is never by producing flowers and fruit.

The main classification of the large seaweeds is by their colour into green, brown and red divisions, although the distinction is not always clear as some brown seaweeds may look green, especially when they are moribund, and some red forms look brown at first sight. The green seaweeds, which are chemically most like land plants, are in general found on the upper parts of the beach. *Enteromorpha*, which has a long, hollow frond containing gasses which cause it to float up to the surface of the water at high tide, can stand extremes of temperature, salinity and desiccation. *Ulva*, or sea lettuce, which looks like a seedling lettuce, is more generally distributed over the middle shore. There are many small green seaweeds, such as the stiff, unbranched *Chaetophora* or the branched *Cladophora*, which form tufts of green in rock pools, while the delicate *Bryopsis* is often found in sheltered places lower on the shore.

Zonation of algae is dependent on light, and the ability to withstand exposure.

splash zone

Pelvetia canaliculata

Fucus spiralis

high water

Fucus vesiculosus

Ascophyllum nodosum

Fucus serratus

Himanthalia elongata

low water

Laminaria spp.

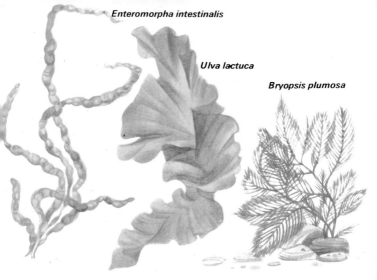

Enteromorpha intestinalis

Ulva lactuca

Bryopsis plumosa

Three common green seaweeds.

Brown algae

The brown seaweeds in general occupy the middle part of the beach. They contain chemicals which enable them to make full use of the reduced light under water. They are not randomly situated, however, and demonstrate a zonation which can be seen more clearly among the wracks than any other group of seaweeds.

On the uppermost part of the beach, sometimes extending into the splash zone, the channel wrack, *Pelvetia caniculata,* may occur. Each frond, which is up to fifteen centimetres long, is incurved at the edges, which gives it a gutter-like section. It may dry out completely to form brittle, black tufts on the rocks, but these return to life when wetted again by the sea. About the level of high water at neap tide, the flat wrack, *Fucus spiralis*, is found. Each frond is twisted towards the base – the reason for its Latin name. Below this, on the upper middle beach, is the bladder wrack, *Fucus vesiculosus*, which is characterized by small, usually paired air bladders, and on the lower middle beach *Fucus serratus* occurs. This is generally larger than the other species and has saw edges to the fronds.

Many other species of brown seaweed inhabit the middle and lower beach. Some of them, such as *Desmarestia* or *Dictyota*, are relatively fragile plants, but many are robustly built and can survive the battering of the sea on exposed coasts. Others, such as the bootlace weed, *Chorda filum,* are slippery due to a secretion of protective mucus which prevents them from drying out at low tide. As the tide retreats to its lowest level, the sinister brown fronds of the oarweeds may be seen. These, the largest British algae, are rarely totally exposed, but they may be torn up and cast on the beach in rough weather.

Although they are abundant, only five species of oarweed occur in British waters. *Laminaria saccharina* has an un-branched, wavy-edged frond, which may be up to three metres long. It has a rather small holdfast and is often attached to small boulders and stones. *Laminaria digitata* has a holdfast of 'rootlets' which fix on to the surface of the rock and grip it so firmly that when a cast-up specimen is examined, it will be seen that it is the surface of the rock which has broken, not the seaweed. The holdfasts of this species and *Laminaria hyperborea*, which are similar, provide secure niches in which many small, soft-bodied animals can survive. *Saccorhiza polyschides* is one of the fastest growing seaweeds, making a frond up to two and a half metres long in a single season. *Alaria esculenta* is smaller and more fragile than the other oarweeds and is found only in extremely exposed, rough places. A new seaweed, related to the tropical Sargassum, has recently been introduced to European waters, probably as part of the packing for Japanese oysters. The spores, released into waters of a suitable temperature, flourished and colonies of this prolific seaweed are now invading the south coast of Britain. Another possible invader is *Macrocystis*, the largest of all seaweeds, which grows to a length of seventy-five metres. It has been suggested that this might be introduced to the Britanny coast to be cultivated for the alginate industry. If this happens it is almost certain to spread beyond the intended area and might have serious effects on the flora and fauna of north-west Europe.

Typical brown seaweeds of a rocky shore.

Fucus spiralis

Pelvetia canaliculata

Laminaria digitata

Himanthalia elongata

Fucus serratus

Saccorhiza polyschides

Red algae

Low down the beach, covered by water for much of the time, are the numerous species of red seaweed. Protected from the battering waves, many of them are small and delicate in structure. They are able to utilize low levels of light and in some cases may even grow in the shadow of the large oarweeds, as does *Rhodymenia*, which may often be seen thriving on the stipes of cast-up species of *Laminaria*.

A few red seaweeds can be found higher up the beach; a common species there is *Porphyra umbilicalis* (see page 35) which can stand considerable desiccation. Some species of red seaweeds are able to absorb calcium salts to such an extent that they develop a stony texture. These plants may form purplish pink encrusting patches in middle and lower shore pools. *Corallina*, which forms upright tufts of articulated branches, hardly looks like a plant at first sight. Some of the red seaweeds may have large, thick fronds; *Dilsea carnosa* and *Phycodrys rubens* (in which each frond is like an elongated oak leaf) are two of the most easily recognized of the larger species.

One of the difficulties in identifying the red seaweeds is the variation in their appearance in different conditions of shelter or exposure. *Chondrus crispus,* a common middle and lower shore seaweed, may form a flat frond which is branched at the tip when it grows in rough water. Under very still conditions, the frond is narrower and thicker and deeply bifurcate at the end. A number of other medium-sized species are bewilderingly similar to each other and can only be identified with certainty by microscopic examination. For instance a handlens will show the curious 'crab claw' tips of the fronds of most species of *Ceramium,* and the curious knotted appearance of the cells which give a banded appearance to the thread-like fronds. Fortunately no magnification is needed to see the beautiful branching pattern of such delicate species as *Plocamium* and *Plumaria* which, although they usually grow low down on the beach or even in sublittoral waters, are very often to be found cast high up on the shore by the force of a storm.

Some of these red seaweeds grow on the rocky shore; others will be washed up from below the tide line.

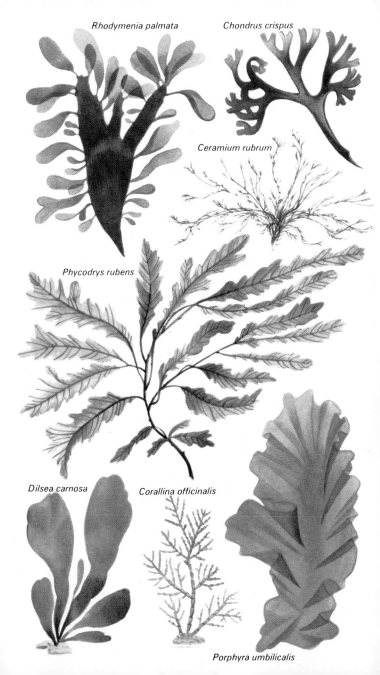

Rhodymenia palmata

Chondrus crispus

Ceramium rubrum

Phycodrys rubens

Dilsea carnosa

Corallina officinalis

Porphyra umbilicalis

Microscopic life and simple shore animals

Much of the life of the seashore is microscopic in size. Floating in with every high tide are millions of tiny animals and plants, collectively known as plankton. Plant plankton includes diatoms and flagellates, such as *Noctiluca*, which may light the sea with their phosphorescence on a summer night. The animals may be creatures such as arrow worms, which remain small for the whole of their lives, or the larvae of many kinds of creatures, which are dispersed in their planktonic phase, but finally settle down to a more or less sedentary adult life.

Many of the inhabitants of the seashore feed on the plankton which they filter out of the water in various ways. Sponges pump this nutritive 'sea soup' through many tiny holes into their honeycomb bodies. It is pumped out again through a smaller number of large holes, giving the common breadcrumb sponge – which encrusts rocks around the shore – the appearance of a patch of tiny volcanoes. The Bryozoa, or moss animals, often form encrusting patches on rocks or large

The food of the crumb-of-bread sponge (1) includes the larvae of the netted whelk (2) and the shore crab (3), both enlarged.

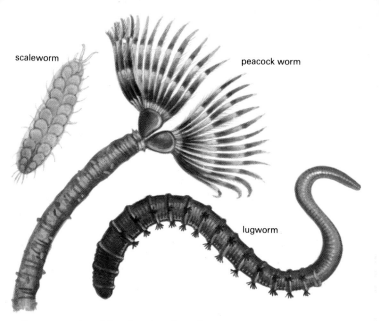

scaleworm

peacock worm

lugworm

Three examples of the diversity of seashore worms.

seaweeds where, after death, their horny skeletons may be obvious. Each lacy spread was the home of a mass of tiny creatures which, with their grabbing tentacles, strained their planktonic food from the water.

On land, worms tend to be dull animals, but this cannot be said about the larger worms of the seashore, which are often brightly coloured and quick in their reactions to hunt or hide from their enemies. They may be free living like the ragworm *Nereis*, which is to be found under large stones at the lower edge of the beach, or they may have a form of protection, either scales or tubes of calcareous material or of cemented sand grains, into which they can retreat at great speed if danger threatens. The handsome, curved shell of the serpulid worm, or the skeleton of a bryozoan may sometimes be of interest to beachcombers in search of decorative natural objects but on the whole, the soft-bodied animals mentioned on this page should be admired for their beauty and then left alone for this cannot be preserved once they are dead.

Sting-celled animals

Many soft-bodied animals are to be found on the beach and are included here so that the beachcomber may recognize what he has found, and may be inspired by their delicate forms to make designs based on his seashore observations.

The most important and obvious of these creatures belong to a group called the Cnidaria, or sting-celled animals. They are soft bodied and generally circular in shape, a feature which indicates an inactive way of life, but they are nevertheless predators. They subdue their prey with minute but numerous sting cells on their tentacles. The commonest cnidarians are the sea anemones, which are to be found on almost every beach. Attached to rocks or breakwaters they look like blobs of jelly at low tide, but when covered with water, they expand their tentacles to the flower-like shape which has given them their name. The first to be seen is likely to be the beadlet anemone which is red or green in colour. The largest British anemone, with a tentacle span of twenty centimetres, is the dahlia anemone, which often lives where there is a rapid flow of water in a channel in the rocks. The beautiful *Sagartia elegans* is usually hidden under an overhang in deeper rock pools and the plumose anemone is often found on pier pilings.

The anemone's tiny relatives, the hydroids, are also abundant on the beach, but they often go unnoticed because of their small size, in spite of the fact that they are usually colonial and live grouped together on the fronds of seaweeds, or on rocks. No European cnidarian is harmful to man, for their prey consists of tiny animals and their sting cells cannot penetrate the skin of a human hand. Jellyfishes are also cnidarians from the open sea, doomed once they come on dry land, but these should generally be avoided for their sting cells can produce a painful rash. The common moon jelly is harmless, but the compass jellyfish and *Cyanea* are unpleasant to handle or even to be touched by. Far more unpleasant is the Portuguese man o' war which is not a true jellyfish but a complex colonial animal of the open sea. If swept up on the beach, it should be avoided at all costs.

Hydroids, sea anemones and jellyfish are among the commoner sting-celled animals.

compass jellyfish

plumose anemone

Sagartia elegans

Hydractinia echinata
on hermit crab shell

snakelocks anemone

Crustaceans

Crabs and lobsters

Insects are the most numerous kind of animals on land, yet strangely they play virtually no part in the life of the sea. A few species may be found on the beach, but these are small and insignificant forms and it is their relatives the crustaceans which are abundant in both species and numbers.

Crustaceans are boneless animals, supported and protected by a hard shell. This does not stretch, nor is it added to as the animal grows, but it must be shed so that another new skin, lying underneath and temporarily able to stretch, may accommodate growth and then harden. This is one of the factors which limits the size of these animals, for during the period of hardening they are at risk from many predators, and must therefore hide and be inactive. In the sea, where their heavy bodies are supported by water, some crustaceans attain a body the size of a small dog, although most are very much smaller than this. On the beach, even the largest crustaceans measure only a few centimetres in length and most are in fact much smaller.

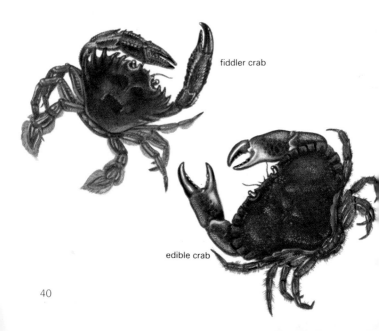

fiddler crab

edible crab

The largest crustaceans are those of the order Decapoda. These have five pairs of walking (or swimming) legs attached to the thorax, the central part of the body. The first pair of these legs always carries claws. In some species, for instance the lobster, they may be of different shapes – one for crushing and the other for tearing food. Lobsters are usually found only on the lower part of the beach in the deep rock pools where, with a flick of their tails, they can shoot backwards into a safe crevice. The crabs, of which there are many kinds, are also heavily armoured but they have short tails tucked under the thorax. The commonest is the shore crab, but small edible crabs are also widespread and velvet swimming crabs may be seen lower down the beach. Intermediate between the lobsters and the true crabs are the squat lobsters, which carry their long abdomens under the body, and the hermit crabs in which the abdomen is long but unarmoured and is tucked into the shell of a dead sea snail for protection.

For the beachcomber the large crustaceans may bring rewards in terms of food, for most are edible, although only one species of crab and lobster are normally eaten in Britain. The cast shells, frequently found on the beach, are often worth collecting for use in decoration.

The hard shells of the larger crustaceans to be found on the shore protect them against their enemies.

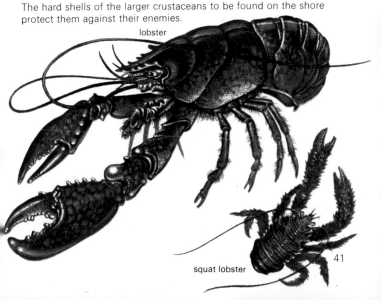

lobster

squat lobster

41

Sandhoppers *(inset)* among the decaying seaweed are a major food for the turnstone.

Shrimps and prawns

The large crustaceans have a host of small relatives, many of which are found on the beach. Some, such as the prawns and true shrimps, are closely related swimming decapods; others are fundamentally different in many ways. Prawns are large (up to twelve centimetres long), with long antennae and a point or rostrum between the eyes. They are creatures of rock pools where there are seaweeds and crevices in which to hide. Shrimps are smaller and have short antennae and no rostrum; they are to be found in a wide range of habitats wherever there is sand against which they can hide their almost transparent bodies. Both prawns and shrimps moult their outer shells as they grow and these may sometimes be found, hanging like ghosts of their former owners, in the still waters of a rock pool. They are too fragile to be preserved dry but could make an interesting challenge to anybody wishing to try a really difficult subject for plastic embedding (see page 98).

Prawns and shrimps are caught for food, but there are many

other small crustaceans on the beach which, while doubtless edible, are normally spared by humans, although their curious shapes and adaptations make them worth searching for. Some are found in rock pools and among floating debris and may be extremely difficult to see, although they are not generally uncommon. These include the opossum shrimps, which match their colour exactly to their background of red and green seaweeds. If one is taken from one coloured background to another it can, after several days, adapt itself perfectly to the new colour. Skeleton shrimps rely on their emaciated shape which merges beautifully with the fronds of the seaweeds and hydroids among which they live. Some small crustaceans, however, may be extremely abundant. Sandhoppers may look like a brown cloud above the beach as they hop about in the wake of the retreating tide, looking for food. They may find a rich feast in piles of decaying seaweed on the shore and are almost always associated with it. Other species make burrows in the sand and feed on minute particles that they find there.

Cunning disguises adopted by many of the smaller crustaceans include transparency, and a body resembling seaweeds.

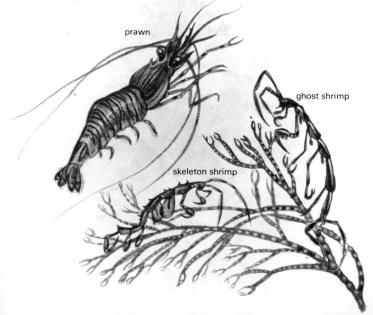

prawn

ghost shrimp

skeleton shrimp

Barnacles

Some of the commonest and most obvious sorts of animals to be seen on the shore are the acorn barnacles which may, in some places, number over thirty thousand to the square metre, or a thousand million to a kilometre length of beach. These heavily armoured creatures look at first sight like molluscs but are in fact crustaceans, a fact which was determined only when their larval life was studied during the last century.

The immature barnacle shows a close similarity to a crab larva, but having developed as part of the plankton, it then changes to a form which merely looks for a place to attach itself on some firm object, such as a rock or breakwater, or even the shell of a limpet. Once such a spot has been discovered, the creature cements itself to it and develops stout, limy plates which protect it from desiccation and from the battering waves. At high tide the central plates are opened and the hairy appendages, which are comparable to the legs of other crustaceans, kick out into the water to comb minute food particles into the barnacle's mouth. There are several species round the coast of Britain, but they may be difficult to identify with certainty.

The beachcomber may well find that a pebble or old shell carrying barnacles is more decorative than one without them,

Attached to rocks or breakwaters, acorn barnacles are abundant on the beach. Goose barnacles are occasionally swept in from the sea.

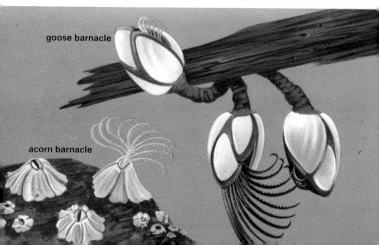

Zonation is clearly shown by the periwinkles.

little periwinkle

rough periwinkle

flat periwinkle

common periwinkle

but apart from this slight aesthetic interest, their small size alone will probably cause them to be ignored.

Molluscs

Periwinkle zonation

The most obvious shelled animals on many beaches are the molluscs. One group of gastropod molluscs, the periwinkles, exhibits zonation particularly well. The little periwinkle is found only at the top of the beach, extending into the splash zone, where it feeds on lichens. The rough periwinkle is found below this and lower still, in the *Fucus vesiculosus* zone, the flat periwinkle occurs, while the large or common periwinkle lives furthest down the beach of all, although it is still above the level of low water at neap tides.

45

Mollusc classification

The creatures most sought after by the beachcomber who wants a decorative reminder of his seaside holiday are the molluscs, which are to be found at all levels on almost all sorts of beach. Their name refers to the fact that they have soft, boneless bodies. They are, however, protected in most cases by a hard shell generally composed of three layers. The outer layer is horny, the middle layer is usually hard and heavy and made of calcium minerals, usually calcite, while the inner layer is pearly. These three layers may vary in their relative thickness; in some of the top shells, for instance, the pearly section is the thickest and may show through on to the outer surface.

The molluscs are divided into a number of classes, which at first look very different from each other, although they are fundamentally similar. Those most likely to be seen first on the average beach are the limpets, which are members of the snail class, or gastropods. They have a simple, conical shell, unlike most of their relatives which have a whorled shell but, in common with them, they have a large, muscular foot on which the animal moves, and similar eyes and tentacles. Limpets, which look so immobile at low tide, graze the growth

of young seaweeds and, as they feed, may move some distance from their home spot, to which they return as the tide falls. A beautiful shell worth hunting for among the oarweeds is the blue-rayed limpet, which gnaws itself a secure notch in these large seaweeds which grow below tide level.

Some gastropods, such as the whelk, are carnivores. Whelks rasp their way into the bodies of their prey with file-like tongues. Cowries are also flesh-eaters, feeding on sponges or bryozoans. Necklace shells are among the most successful of predators. Although large and rounded, they plough through the sand below the surface until they meet a bivalve, which is unable to escape as the snail surrounds it with its huge foot. Bivalve shells with a small hole neatly bored in them may often be picked up on the beach – evidence that they have been victims of the necklace shell. Some gastropods have lost their shells, but unlike their dull-coloured land counterparts, the sea slugs are among the most beautiful and bizarre animals of the beach.

Apart from the gastropods there are, of course, other molluscs to be found on the beach. The little chiton, with its jointed shell, lives on the underside of rocky overhangs, or in similar sheltered spots. Tusk shells are members of another

cuttle bone

whelk egg cases

whelk

necklace shell

mussels attached
by byssus threads

cockles

tusk shell

Tusk shells and bivalve molluscs, which often burrow below the sand, may live in dense communities.

small group, the scaphopods, which are sand burrowers, rarely met with alive, although their tusk-shaped shells are cast up in some places. Another group, which is truly marine, includes the octopus, which may make its lair at the lowest level of the tide but cannot tolerate any desiccation. Its oceanic relatives, the squids, are rarely seen ashore, but cuttlefish may sometimes be seen in large, lower shore pools with a sandy bottom, and after spring storms in particular the hard, white, internal body supports of thousands of these animals may be cast ashore. This is known as cuttlebone, although it is far removed from true bone in its structure.

The most important group of molluscs, apart from the gastropods, is the lamellibranchs, or bivalves. As their name suggests, they have a double shell, which is hinged so that it can be opened or tightly shut. Although dense mussel beds may be seen on the beach, bivalves generally live under the sand. The large foot, so characteristic of the snail-like molluscs, is transformed in bivalves into a digging organ. Some bivalves are difficult to catch alive, for they can dig more efficiently

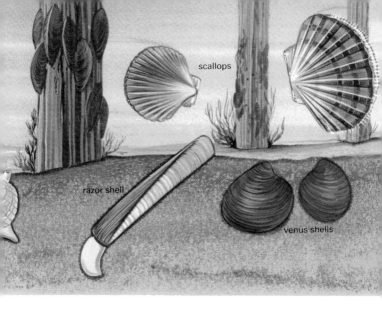

scallops

razor shell

venus shells

than most humans. Shore-living lamellibranchs feed at high tide, at which time they push a pair of tubes or siphons to the surface of the sand. Sea water is drawn in through one of these, pumped over the gills, and then leaves through the other. This action allows the animals to breathe and feed simultaneously, for bivalves are plankton feeders and the minute, floating fragments of life are trapped on a mucous band, from where they are taken to the stomach at the same time as the oxygen is removed from the water by the gills.

This seems to be a very efficient way of life, as may be judged by the numbers of bivalves which are estimated to be able to survive in a small area – over 1,000 to a square metre in ideal conditions. Several species may be present in the same area, living at different depths and having siphons of different lengths to allow them to feed on the limitless plankton of the summer months. A clue to their abundance may sometimes be seen after a summer storm, when the churning waves disturb the sand and throw millions of cockles, venus shells and other bivalves on to the beach.

Echinoderms and sea squirts

The echinoderms are limited by their structure to a life in the sea and are unable to stand desiccation or freshwater conditions. All echinoderms are radially symmetrical – usually with a pentamerous symmetry – and most are sluggish and slow moving. The hallmark of the echinoderms is their *tube feet,* which are like water-filled balloons, provided in most cases with suckers. The animals use them in locomotion, although some are sensory and may also have some other specialized function.

Like the molluscs, echinoderms can be divided into several classes which are superficially dissimilar. The most familiar of those found on the beach are the starfishes, which live under cover of stones or seaweed on the lower shore. The tough and sometimes spiny skin of the starfish overlies an extremely flexible body, supported internally by a skeleton of limy rods.

Sea urchins enclose themselves in spiny, calcareous plates, perforated to allow protrusion of the tube feet. Some burrow below the sand; others live in deep pools which never dry out; others live below the tide line, but even so their shells are sometimes thrown up on to the shore. They feed on scraps of seaweed and debris, which they masticate with a powerful jaw system known as *'Aristotle's lantern'*. This is sometimes found more or less intact and is one of the most intriguing and decorative objects from the beach. Brittle stars and sea cucumbers are other classes of echinoderms to be found between the tides, but neither is likely to appeal to the beachcomber for the brittle star, as its name suggests, is extremely fragile and the sea cucumber is a sluggish, soft-bodied animal.

Although they are related to the vertebrates and have a tadpole-like larva with an internal body support, sea squirts are also soft-bodied animals. They may be solitary or colonial creatures, such as the common golden star sea squirt, but in both cases they draw large amounts of sea water over an internal gill basket, extracting food and oxygen in the process.

Starfishes and their relatives are common on the lower shore; some sea squirts also occur higher up the beach.

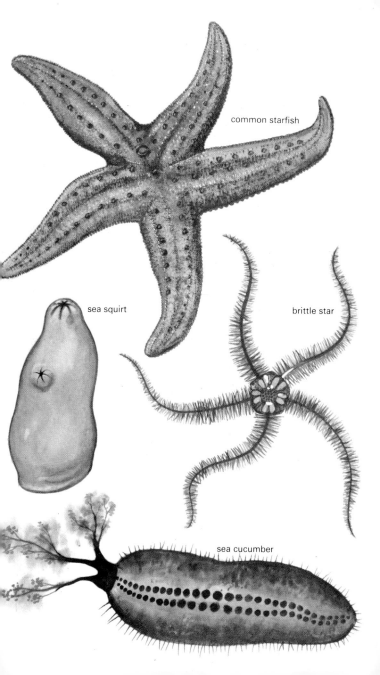

common starfish

sea squirt

brittle star

sea cucumber

Shore fishes

Many small fishes are to be found on the shore. Unlike some of the invertebrates, which can tolerate periods of exposure, fishes are bound to remain in more or less moist conditions throughout the period of low tide. They are therefore found in rock pools, or hidden under seaweed where they can keep cool and damp, or buried in sand where the tide has left a shallow pool of water behind. The battering waves present a problem which the fishes have overcome in many cases by modifying the pelvic fins to form suckers, with which they can hang on to rocks and withstand even severe storms.

The flatfishes are probably the most frequently encountered of those species which hide in sand. Spawned in shallow water and hatching as symmetrically shaped fry, they migrate inshore where, as they grow, they develop an asymmetry and become flattened. Thus they lie on one side, the lower eye moving to the upper side of the head. At low tide they bury themselves in the sand in shallow pools and, although quite numerous, may be quite invisible due to their power of altering their colour to match that of their surroundings. Sand eels, as their name suggests, also bury themselves as do weever fishes.

Seashore fishes may be found in rock pools, hidden under seaweed or buried in the sand.

wrasse

lumpsucker

52

Sucker fishes of various kinds inhabit the beach clinging, like the lumpsucker, to rocks or stones, where their smooth, large-headed shapes make little break in the rush of water as it flows over them. A few grow quite large – the Cornish lumpsucker has been recorded at over sixty centimetres in length – but most are small. Wrasse are frequently large fish and are usually brightly coloured. They sometimes curve their thickset bodies round a projecting rock and are very difficult to dislodge since the whole body has become, in effect, a clinging sucker.

Most of the shore fishes are slow moving and their food is to be found among the small animals of the beach. Many of them wrench barnacles or small bivalves from the rocks, using their remarkably powerful teeth and jaws. Many also have a degree of parental care unusual in fishes in general. It is often the males which protect the eggs, although in the viviparous blenny they develop internally in the body of the female; when they hatch, the fry measure about three centimetres in length and are able to colonize the beach immediately, without an intervening planktonic phase.

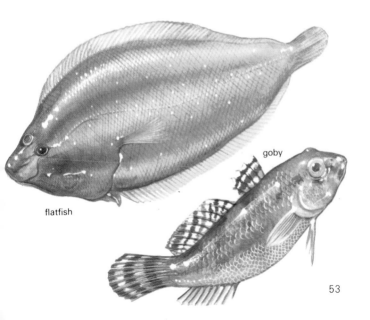

goby

flatfish

Fish egg cases and other remains

Although beach fishes are numerous in some areas, they are few in number compared with fishes of the open sea. We are, however, reminded of these by objects of many kinds which are to be found on the beach. Probably those most frequently found are the egg cases of various small sharks. Unlike the bony fishes which mostly spawn huge numbers of unprotected eggs into the sea, sharks and their relatives either produce living young, or lay a small number of large, yolky eggs protected in a horny case. These may take a considerable time to hatch and the empty cases are then cast up on the shore. Those of the spotted dogfish have curled tendrils at each corner by which the egg cases were anchored to seaweeds offshore. The egg cases of various species of ray may also be found; these have points instead of tendrils at the corners.

Other remains of shark-like fishes which may sometimes be found are the tooth-like skin 'bucklers' of rays, and the horny, sharp spines of the piked dogfish. These may be the remains of fishes thrown aside by fishermen, which have then been carried for some distance by scavenging gulls, thus along with other food remains they may occur on cliff tops, well above sea level. The teeth of some fishes may also occur on the beach. Puzzling objects sometimes found are the pharyngeal or 'throat' teeth of the wrasse. They are small, hard and rounded and those of the lower jaw are on a T-shaped bone which must be one of the least destructible parts of the fish, for it is part of the apparatus used for crushing the shells of the animals on which the wrasse feeds. The small bones of fishes are rarely found, for they disintegrate soon after death, but the central part of the vertebrae may survive to be found. These may be recognized by their rounded, biconcave shape and the lines radiating from the centre to the edge of the bone.

Other objects which occasionally turn up on the beach are the markers placed on fishes by research workers concerned with problems of their longevity or migrations. These metal or plastic tags carry details of the authority to be informed, and there may be a small reward for the finder for adding to the total of our knowledge about fish.

The beachcomber looking for unusual objects may welcome

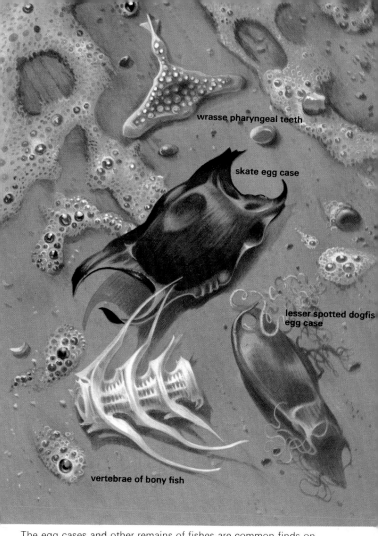

The egg cases and other remains of fishes are common finds on many beaches.

a find of fish bones or teeth, but on the whole they do not represent a major part of beach debris and are not sufficiently decorative to be searched for to the exclusion of everything else.

55

Birds

Many kinds of bird may be found on the seashore, although some of them are only temporary residents there. Cliff-nesting jackdaws, for instance, discover the rich pickings of the beach, especially where there are people. For gulls, however, this is a regular way of life for these are not birds of the open sea but rather inshore scavengers, never neglecting any source of food. They sometimes dig bivalves from the sand and fly with them to a nearby rock or even a road, where they drop the shells so that they can get at the succulent flesh inside. They will also feed on all sorts of waste and in springtime, on the eggs and young of other birds. When not feeding, the birds spend much of their time resting, or preening. It is often possible to see where a group of birds has been sitting, especially at moulting time, for the beach will be littered with feathers tweaked out in the course of grooming.

A collection of such feathers will show – due to the differences in shape and colour – that many birds beside gulls may be resting on the shore. One bird seen commonly is the smart black and white oystercatcher, a bird which feeds not on oysters, but on small bivalves. These are probed from the sand and deftly opened by the long, orange beak, which is clearly visible as the bird flies whistling away from the danger

tern

of human presence. Oystercatchers belong to a large group of birds known as waders, which all have long beaks and legs and may be seen – particularly in the wintertime – on muddy shores and estuaries, where their three-toed footprints may be easily recognized.

Terns make use of the beach in the summertime for breeding. Their nests are shallow scrapes in sand or gravel and the eggs, which resemble pebbles, are difficult to see. Above all other birds, nesting terns should be left alone for they are easily disturbed and the eggs are then often destroyed by predators such as foxes, gulls or rats.

Several species of auk, including puffins, guillemots and razorbills occur round the coast of Britain, where they nest in remote cliffed areas. These dumpy, short-winged birds are oceanic and spend as little time as possible on land, catching their food under water. Naturally, they have to breathe at frequent intervals and all too often surface into a patch of spilt oil. They almost always die as a result of this and the populations of auks have declined greatly in recent years. In many cases the pathetic remains are washed up on the beach where the oil and soft parts eventually disappear and the skeleton, bleached by the waves and recognized by its lightness of weight, may be found by the beachcomber.

A few of the many birds likely to be encountered on the shore.

little auk

oiled puffin

Loggerhead turtle.

Amphibians and reptiles

Amphibians are generally animals of fresh water, but one European species, the natterjack toad, is sometimes found near the coast, surviving there because of the large amount of mucus with which the skin is protected. Occasionally it spawns in brackish pools in the splash zone, although it is uncertain just how much salinity the animal can stand. Although it often lives near to the sea, there is no record of the natterjack toad feeding on shore invertebrates such as shrimps or sandhoppers but rather on small insects and spiders. It is possible that at least some of these may be individuals which have been blown into salt water; beetles in particular may often be seen struggling to escape from pools into which they have dropped accidentally. Such animals would make easy prey for the natterjack toad.

Millions of years ago many sorts of reptiles lived in the sea and some of these must have come ashore to lay their eggs, although there were others which could produce living young in the water. Even so, some of these were sometimes stranded in shallow water and many museums have the remains of such creatures (some collected by Mary Anning) in their possession. Today, however, most reptiles are animals of land or fresh water, and the species that do inhabit the sea

Natterjack toad.

are tropical in their distribution. They include some crocodiles, and marine turtles, the sea snakes and, on the Galápagos Islands, some iguanas which have taken to life at the edge of the sea. The crocodiles and iguanas are never found very far from the land to which they must return to lay their eggs. The sea snakes are ovo-viviparous and produce a small number of large, well-developed young capable of swimming and finding their food in the seas off the coasts of South-east Asia where they are born.

Only the marine turtles range widely throughout the oceans, mainly in tropical latitudes. They must return to land to lay their eggs, but at other times may be seen far from their breeding beaches, sometimes in temperate waters and occasionally coming ashore on the coasts of Britain or western Europe. The leathery turtle, which measures up to three metres in length has been reported a good many times from British waters, or on beaches, and the smaller loggerhead turtle and Kemp's ridley turtle have both been recorded with certainty. The chances of seeing a turtle round the coasts of Europe are slight, but it is a possibility. If you think that you have seen one report it to the local coastguard who will know the correct procedure for dealing with the information.

Mammals

Seals are marine mammals which have to come on to land to produce their young. Two species are still fairly common round western Europe: the common or harbour seal and the Atlantic or grey seal. The former is found in general round lowland coasts where there are sandy beaches, while the latter prefers rocky skerries and islands on which to rest and reproduce. Because of the general controversy surrounding seals, a good deal of research is being carried out on their lives and habits, and the pups born in some places are banded with metal rings placed on one of the hind toes. Should you find a seal pup carrying such a tag you will contribute materially to the studies by informing the bander, whose name and address will be on it.

Whales are completely marine creatures and cannot survive if they become beached, which seems to happen particularly on shelving, sandy shores. Pilot whales seem to get stranded more frequently than other species, and in the past schools

Left Stranded pilot whale. *Right* Grey seal and calf. The calf has almost replaced the white coat it had at birth.

of these whales would be driven into very shallow water where they could easily be killed for winter food supplies. This form of whaling is no longer practised, but almost every year a few whales drive themselves ashore to die. Records of such strandings are kept at the British Museum (Natural History). Any whales found stranded should be reported at once to the local coastguard, who will pass the information on to the relevant authorities. Apart from truly marine mammals, some land mammals may use the shore occasionally. Otters may find fishing easy in the pools and runnels of the beach, and other predators such as foxes and stoats are often present, especially when the seabirds are nesting.

Domestic animals are sometimes grazed on the seashore or on the saltings within the splash zone, and the bones of livestock – especially cattle – are quite often found with the strandline debris. Bleached quite white after a long period in the sea, these are often attractive objects in their own right and may make a souvenir for the beachcomber.

BEACH CONSERVATION AND BEACH POLLUTION

In general the beachcomber is concerned with the debris and chance findings of the shore, and not with collecting living plants or animals. Anybody wishing to take living organisms from the beach should remember the *Seashore Code*, published by the National Environment Research Council, which reminds us to look, but not to destroy.

Certain seashore animals, however, are used as food and are taken alive, although comparatively few are regularly used as food in Britain. Those that are, are mostly so abundant that there is little danger of their becoming extinct through over-collecting and some, such as shrimps and flatfishes, do not seem to suffer even through commercial exploitation. At one time seabirds' eggs were collected as food and it was estimated that up to sixty percent of any one year's eggs could be taken from a colony without affecting the numbers of birds over the years. This trade has largely stopped and it is now illegal to collect the eggs of most birds, although gulls' eggs may be taken in some places.

Scarcity and illegality apart, there is one other important point to consider when collecting food from the shore and this

Collecting shellfish near a sewer outfall may result in a severe bout of food poisoning.

Always collect seafood on a clean beach.

is pollution, which can make many sea creatures dangerous to eat. Industrial pollution, which may be the result of discharging waste containing heavy metals into the water may, in extreme cases, kill all of the animals in the area. Often, however, they survive with a high level of poisonous wastes in their bodies. Anybody eating them concentrates the poisons still further and although it is unlikely that eating winkles or mussels collected on holiday could have any very serious results, it is better not to take the risk if you think that industrial pollution is present.

Another type of pollution is unfortunately all too common in many places where crude sewage is discharged into the sea. Often the minerals from this enrich the water so that plants and animals grow particularly well in the region of the outfall pipe, but the animals may carry disease organisms of many kinds, which are not always destroyed by cooking. A third type of pollution affects mussels in particular. At certain times a natural poison produced by tiny organisms becomes concentrated in their food. An indication not to gather mussels would be a number of dead animals on the shore – especially birds and fishes – which could have been killed by the same poison. If you observe the signs of pollution and still gather and eat seashore animals, you are running the risk of serious illness.

FOOD FROM THE BEACH

Seashore plants as food

The plants of the seashore may in many cases be eaten, although the nutritive value of seaweed at least is low for the carbohydrates which they contain cannot easily be broken down and digested by man or other mammals. Anybody considering collecting seaweeds for food should be certain that the area is free from industrial pollution. In any case, before eating any seaweed, it should be washed carefully in fresh water to get rid of the grit and small animals which may be attached to it. Several sorts of seaweed are eaten in many parts of the world and one species of *Porphyra* is cultivated for food round the shores of Japan. A closely related form is collected in Britain, especially in the south-west and south Wales where, after boiling, it may be made into a sauce to be eaten with mutton. When mixed with oatmeal and fried it is known as *laver bread*.

Because of the difficulty of naming seaweeds accurately there is some confusion about the actual species which may be used for a particular purpose but one commonly eaten in Britain is *Rhodymenia palmata* which is roughly dried and eaten as an appetizer, especially in some parts of Ireland where it is known as *dulse. Carragheen* is the name given to *Chondrus*

Many seaweeds are edible and may be eaten raw or cooked.

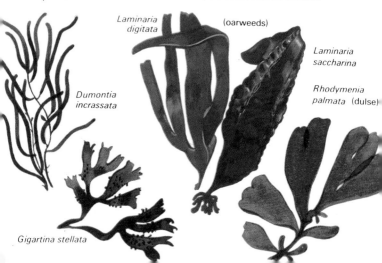

Laminaria digitata (oarweeds)

Laminaria saccharina

Dumontia incrassata

Rhodymenia palmata (dulse)

Gigartina stellata

Three of the rooted seashore plants that are often eaten.

crispus, often mixed with *Gigartina stellata,* both of which may be found commonly on middle shore levels. These, after washing, are stewed gently with milk and flavouring to make a blancmange. Almost all of the other common shore seaweeds could be similarly used, although in some cases they may be eaten raw, as for example the young stipes of *Laminaria saccharina* which taste sweet and nutty, and the sea lettuce which has been used as a salad, although it is inclined to be tough and is better boiled. Many foods, however, contain seaweed derivatives, especially alginates, which are mainly used as gelling agents. These are obtained chiefly from oarweeds, which are harvested in some places.

Many of the flowering plants of the shore can also be eaten. The sea pea, which grows on shingle beaches, can make a refreshing snack on a hot day. Glasswort, which grows at the lower edges of salt marshes, can be eaten raw if picked young; or cooked like asparagus or pickled if gathered when mature. Rock samphire may be eaten boiled, but is more usually pickled.

Seashore animals as food

The choicest seafood animals are mostly to be found below the tideline, since oysters, scallops and the large lobsters generally live in deep water offshore. Small lobsters and edible crabs may be found under rocks on the lower shore but lobsters, which have suffered from over fishing, may not be taken below the length of ten centimetres nor may females carrying eggs be collected for food. Prawns and shrimps can be caught on the shore using a net with a bar which disturbs the animals as they lie hidden in the sand. One of the largest commercial shrimp fisheries is on the wide sands of Morecambe Bay, England, where large nets are dragged across the sands at low tide. At one times horses were trained for this arduous task, but now tractors are used.

Cockle fishing is less highly organized in general, but wide, sandy beaches may still provide a source of food and income. The cockle beds are worked over with a short-handled, blunt-toothed rake, exposing the molluscs which are usually only

Below and *Opposite* Many of the harvests of the sea, commonly bought in shops, are those which you can find for yourself on the beach.

about eight centimetres below the surface, and which are then picked up. Deep burrowing bivalves such as gapers, the larger tellin shells and even razor shells may be eaten. In all cases they should be washed several times in both sea and fresh water and then left for a few hours in salted water to rid themselves of any grit which they might contain. Mussels attach themselves in dense beds to places where the strong flow of water will bring them food. They should be washed in several changes of clean water and kept for some hours before cooking. Winkles, which can be collected from the rocks almost anywhere, can be boiled and eaten straight away.

Limpets may also be eaten, although tastes vary as to the best way to prepare them, some people preferring to eat them raw, straight from the shells, while others insist that only four hours' boiling can make them palatable. Although limpets may be detached easily enough if surprised by a sharp blow, gathering enough of these tightly clamped molluscs to make a worthwhile meal can be a tiring business, and the shore fishes probably offer a more attractive prospect. Even the sand eels, which although small are easily obtained in some places, make excellent eating.

PEBBLES AND STONES

Collecting pebbles and stones

There must be few visitors to the seaside who have not at some time brought home a few pebbles picked up on the beach. When shining wet in the retreating tide, marks and banding show up clearly to give them all an attractive appearance, but once dry many revert to a dull, grey colour, which is a disappointment after their first promise. To avoid this you should aim to limit your searches to beaches where you can expect certain types of pebbles to be found. To begin with, it is useful to consult a geological map so that you will know the sort of pebbles likely to occur on a particular beach. A heavy penknife can be used to test the hardness of specimens, which is often a clue to their identity, and with it you can also scrape at the dull patina which forms over the surface of many types of pebble. For the enthusiast a light geological hammer with which to remove chips from the larger specimens, so that these may be examined under a handlens, is a must.

Along the south coast of Britain the vast majority of pebbles are made of flint, which is a hard, blackish stone, although on the beach the surface is usually grey or white in colour. More interesting pebbles are found mostly on the northern and western beaches, where the hinterland is often made of old or volcanic rocks. It is here that agates and cairngorms (two of the semiprecious stones) can be found commonly, although at first sight on the beach they bear little resemblance to the polished pebble which will probably be the finished product. Some pebbles have a relatively limited distribution, others such as serpentine or jasper, are not generally common but are widespread.

Some pebbles have travelled long distances from their point of origin before being washed up on the beach where you find them. Amber, for instance, which sometimes occurs on the coast of eastern England, is a fossil resin, formed in Scandinavia and carried across the North Sea. Very large pieces have been found occasionally but generally only small fragments survive for amber, in common with jet which is a kind of fossil wood, is a very soft material, quickly broken down by contact with harder stones.

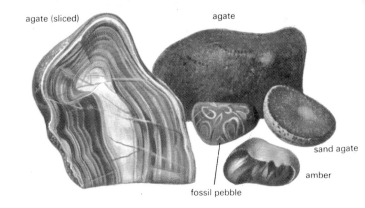

agate (sliced)

agate

sand agate

amber

fossil pebble

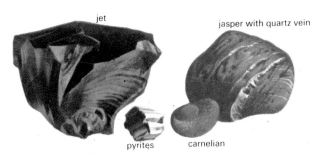

jet

jasper with quartz vein

pyrites

carnelian

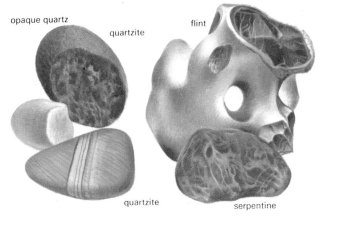

opaque quartz

quartzite

flint

quartzite

serpentine

Varnishing and tumbling stones

The pocketful of pebbles which you have brought back with you from your seaside visit will probably give you pleasure as a reminder of the holiday, but without their wet shine many pebbles look very dull and drab. One way to replace part, at least, of the appearance which first attracted you on the beach is to coat the stone with a clear varnish. The best type comes in an aerosol pack, so that you can spray a very thin layer of varnish which will obscure none of the shape or texture of the pebble. Large stones are best treated in this way, for the tumbling method is not usually practicable for them. It has the advantage that you lose none of the specimen and if you wish you can remove the shine at any time with a solvent.

In recent years many people have taken up the hobby of pebble polishing. For this you will need to buy a pebble tumbler, which is basically a small barrel rotated by an electric motor. Inside the barrel the pebbles tumble against each other and are cut by an abrasive grit which is added. The mutual pounding reduces and rounds the pebbles in the first instance and in later treatment polishes them. Before you begin to polish your pebbles, they should be sorted carefully, for they should all be roughly equal in size and hardness. It is a good

A tumble polisher with *(right)* some tumbled pebbles.

flawed pebbles — discard

idea to break off any awkwardly projecting fragments or any badly flawed pieces, using a hammer and cold chisel. You will be repaid for this tedious job by better shaped, flawless stones.

For the best results, the tumbler barrel should be filled about two-thirds full of pebbles – you cannot do just one or two at a time – then silicon carbide grit should be added in a ratio of 1:10 by weight, and the container filled with water. The first grinding lasts from seven to ten days and the pebbles should be shaped by this treatment, and will also lose about fifty percent of their size. If you are satisfield with the shapes that they have developed, you can proceed to the next stage which smooths the stones using a finer grade of abrasive, and which also lasts for about seven to ten days. Finally, after further washing and sorting, the pebbles are ready for the polishing stage, for which it is best to use a separate barrel since some coarse grit is bound to be embedded in the walls of the shaping and smoothing containers and this would scratch your finished article. Cerium oxide or tin oxide is the abrasive used in the polishing phase, which lasts five to seven days. At the end of this time the pebbles should have an even, high shine and they are now ready to be used in ornaments or decorations.

tumbled pebbles

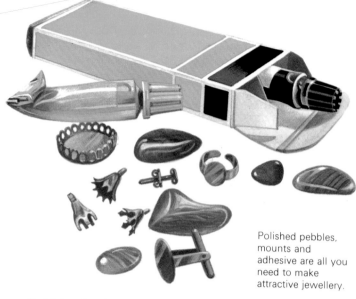

Polished pebbles, mounts and adhesive are all you need to make attractive jewellery.

Pebbles in decoration and jewellery

Once you have varnished or tumble-polished your pebbles, they can be put to some useful or decorative purpose. Large polished stones can make attractive doorstops, but only a limited number of these is needed in most households so, although you may be tempted by a particularly beautiful small boulder for such a purpose, it is better in general to collect small pebbles and fragments which can be polished and stored easily.

You may wish to make a scientific collection of your finds. For this the same sort of trays can be used as those suggested for fossils (see page 83), but the arrangement for the collection can be made on the basis of similar stones; for instance all of the agates stored together, all the carnelians stored together, and so on. In other words, each grouped with its chemical relatives. Another possibility is that you make your collection a geographical one, so that in each block of boxes you have specimens from a particular locality; those from the Lizard in Cornwall in one block, those from, say, Mull or Brittany in another.

As with all collections the value is very much enhanced if

each specimen is properly labelled. However good your memory, details of when and where a specimen was collected will be forgotten unless written down at the time. It is a good idea to put a polished and an unpolished specimen from the same locality together, so that you will be reminded of the appearance of the pebble when you first found it.

Many people, however, will not be content to leave their collection in boxes to be inspected occasionally, but will want to do something more constructive with it. One of the most attractive ways of displaying pebbles is to mount the prettier specimens so that they can be worn as jewellery. Depending on both your degree of dexterity and your interest, the type of jewellery that you make can vary widely from something quickly and cheaply made, to objects which eventually have a considerable intrinsic worth. Today it is no longer necessary to drill stones for making bracelets or earrings, for it is possible to buy metal mounts into which the stones can be stuck, using recently developed adhesives such as epoxy resins, which have great strength and thus minimize the danger of losing the stone from its setting.

cairngorm (coloured quartz)

pendant cut from quartz

A pendant cut from coloured quartz. Veins of this quartz are
sometimes found exposed in rocks near to the sea.

If you feel more ambitious about your jewellery making,
you may wish to use your most prized specimens in a setting
made of precious metal. There are many techniques for this
and the best way to learn is to attend one of the many courses
in jewellery making held in art schools and colleges, or as
evening classes throughout the country. An advantage of this
is that you may learn techniques and use tools such as the one
which cut the quartz in the pendant illustrated. In this, large
quartz crystals have been gem cut using equipment that an
amateur would not normally possess.

You can take your crystals to a lapidary to be cut so that you
then merely have the task of setting them, but if you can do the
whole job yourself the satisfaction in the finished object is
likely to be all the greater. Cutting of this kind is not a suitable
treatment for the majority of beach finds, many of which can
instead be fashioned into cabochons which, when mounted,
can be very pleasing to wear. Should you have a particularly
prized specimen which you feel you cannot do justice to, you
will find that there are many professional craftsmen-jewellers
who will design a setting for your stone. You may find that

your pebble has become part of a work of art which will not only give you pleasure to wear, but which may have considerable value.

Pebbles pictures

A use for pebbles which have been collected in some quantity is to make pebble pictures. These can be quite simple but still very effective decorations. A piece of hardboard makes a suitable backing and the design should first be sketched on this. The pebbles should be sorted for size and colour and should be thoroughly washed in fresh water and dried before you start work. If you wish to use the occasional polished or varnished pebble, this may highlight some points of the design, but in general this is a method of using pebbles with curious markings or shapes which can be worked into the texture of the picture. One of the hard-setting modern adhesives should be used, but each pebble should have only a tiny dab of adhesive before being set in place. It is best to handle your pebbles with small tweezers, which will reduce the chance of getting sticky fingers and spreading glue everywhere.

Driftwood and seaweed may be incorporated in pebble pictures.

SAND

Collecting sand

The idea of collecting sand does not occur to many people probably because it is unusual for sands to differ much in their appearance over quite a wide area. They do vary, however, and an interesting collection can be made which has the advantage, not shared by many other collections, of taking up

Coloured sands can be stored in polythene bags until used to make decorative paperweights.

coloured sands stored in plastic bags

relatively little space, for it can be housed in small tubes or spice jars.

On the beach the sand can be scooped into a plastic bag, but before it is stored it should be washed in a shallow dish in several rinses of fresh water. This will remove a good deal of the salt and the living organisms which are still attached to the sand grains. After washing, the sand should be dried completely preferably in a slow oven. After this, it can be poured into the receptacles in which it is to be stored. Labels with full data as to where the specimen came from and when it was collected should be attached to each jar without obscuring the actual specimen, so that you are able to see at a glance how greatly sands vary in colour and texture from place to place.

Making sand pictures

You may find that your sand collection is pleasing enough in itself and that the dark sands from basalt areas and those shining with grains of mica from beaches backed by granite rocks contrast interestingly with each other and need no further treatment. You may, however, feel inclined to make something decorative from your collection. A large tube, such as a spaghetti jar, can be filled with layers of sands of varying thickness and colour. The decorative effect depends to some extent on the contrast between the layers and you should let one layer settle properly, tapping the side of the jar gently to help it, before adding the next. This is very necessary for if the sand is not well compacted it will gradually settle itself, and the finer grains will work their way downwards muddling up the pattern that you originally created. Your spaghetti jar will have a decorative use only; smaller containers can be filled and used as paperweights.

Another use of sand is to make sand pictures. For this, as for the pebble picture, a piece of hardboard or very stiff card makes the best base. As before, the design should be drawn carefully on the board – an abstract pattern often makes a good sand picture – but if you prefer something representational, remember the limitations of the colours that you have available. The glue that you use need not have the strength required to hold pebbles in place but it should be fairly liquid, for when you have decided just which colour and texture of sand you intend to use for a particular space, paint it with your adhesive and sift the sand over the area, using a small sieve like a tea-strainer. Tip off any surplus and return it if possible to its jar – you may need it in the future. Give each colour time to harden before applying the next, so you will not get your colours mixed unintentionally. If your picture is a large or complex one it will take some time to complete, but try not to rush the job for the end product can be very pleasing. You may feel that you wish to highlight some areas and this can be done by spraying with thin varnish, which will add some degree of shine as well as fixing the grains more securely in place.

Sand pictures are another attractive way of displaying your collection.

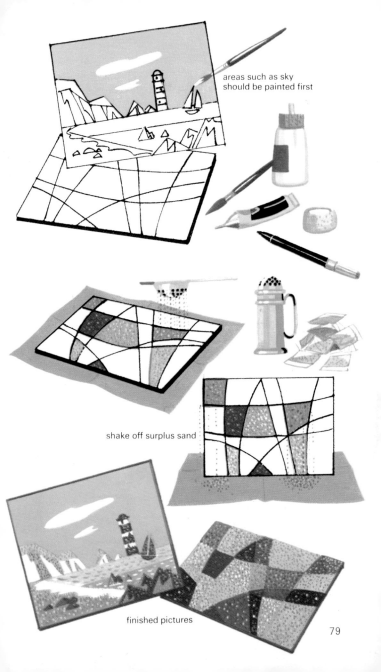

areas such as sky should be painted first

shake off surplus sand

finished pictures

79

FOSSILS

Looking for fossils

Beaches are one of the best places to collect fossils because the action of the waves is constantly exposing fresh specimens. In some places the work of exposing and sorting the fossils is done by the water (see page 20) and in others, where the rock is harder, it is necessary to look for and remove them for yourself.

If, on a seaside holiday, you decide to collect fossils, how can you have the best chance of success? Firstly, it is helpful to have made preparations beforehand, so that you know what you are likely to find. Study a geological map, which will give you a general picture of the structure of the area. Geological maps on a scale of one inch to a mile are now available for almost the whole of Britain and these will prove invaluable to you. The Institute of Geological Sciences also produces a series

Fossil collecting equipment.

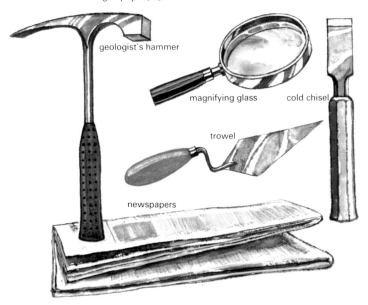

of regional guides to the different areas of Britain and these are very helpful; it is well worth obtaining a copy of the guide which covers the area that you intend to visit. Your study of the map will tell you the type of rock you are likely to meet at any particular place, so you will be able to modify the equipment that you take accordingly. If, for example, you intend to collect fossils from the Headon Beds on the Isle of Wight you will need a small trowel so that you can dig the fossils from the soft cliffs, but this would be useless if you wanted to look for specimens hidden in harder rocks. For these you would need a geological hammer. This is a fairly lightweight tool with one end of the head square faced and the other shaped like a short pick. A geological hammer is an expensive tool to buy, but do not regard it as an unnecessary luxury for it is made of specially tempered steel and will not shatter when used on hard rock, which a cheap household hammer might well do. Do not buy a heavier hammer than you need – it will only add to the weight that you have to carry and most fossils are heavy enough on their own. A small cold chisel is a useful implement to take and may help you to extract specimens more neatly than with a hammer alone.

Depending on the locality, you may have to search in either the cliffs or on the beach for your fossils. It may take you a little while to get your eye in, especially where specimens are rare, but you should soon have some finds to your credit. The excitement of finding a fossil should not prevent you from pausing and dealing with each specimen as it is found. Your hunting equipment should not stop short at the tools for extracting specimens from the rocks, but should include the wherewithal for packing and carrying them in such a way that they will not be damaged. The best material is newspaper, in which your specimens can be wrapped and on which information as to where they were collected can be written in non-run ink. This is most important, for the value of your collection will depend to a large extent on the data associated with the specimens and should include the date and the locality described in as much detail as possible. You will then need something to carry your finds home in; a lightweight rucksack is best, for in this the packets of fossils will fit comfortably and can be carried easily.

A fossil collection

Once you have brought your fossils safely home you will want to examine them in detail, and to classify and store them. For this you will need a handlens and a book which will help you to identify them; there are many on the market and some are suggested in the bibliography. If you find a fossil embedded in a piece of rock, it may be worth carrying the rock home to chip the fossil out at your leisure. For this you will need small chisels, or even mounted needles to scratch away at the remaining rock. When you have amassed a large collection of fossils you may find it useful to house them in trays or cabinets.

In the early stages all that you need are small cabinets with drawers which are as airtight as possible. Since most of your finds will be relatively small objects, a good idea is to use one of the banks of drawers which are sold in most do-it-yourself shops to house screws, washers, etc. As you put the specimens away, each should be carefully labelled and should carry the following information: 1. Identification. 2. Place where collected, giving height up cliff, or level of beach. 3. Date when collected. 4. Name of collector. 5. A serial number. This number is very important and should be written on the specimen as well, so that if the fossil and the label do become separated, they can easily be reunited.

Your collection should be looked at fairly frequently. One reason for this is that many fossils from seashore localities contain a mineral called pyrites. This, under damp atmospheric conditions, can change and break down forming among other things, sulphuric acid, which will destroy the specimen completely and will infect others in the collection. Prevention is of course better than cure and if your collection includes specimens from an area where pyrites occurs, it is best to wash any that you think might be pyritic very thoroughly, preferably leaving them in a bowl with a tap running gently on them all night. They should then be dried, preferably in an oven with a temperature of not more than 70°C, and after this sprayed all over with a thin, protective varnish.

Even after this you should inspect your collection to be certain that the treatment has worked. If, as you open a drawer, you can smell acid and can see a yellow powder forming on a specimen, this is an indication that it is breaking down and you must remove it quickly and neutralize it. This you can do by placing household ammonia (in a small dish) and the fossil together in a tightly closed plastic bag. The yellow powder will turn brown as it is neutralized by the fumes. After a few days you can brush it away, then dry your specimen again in an oven and respray. With luck, the pyrites rot will have been stopped and your specimen will remain intact.

A cabinet with drawers is a useful way of keeping fossils.

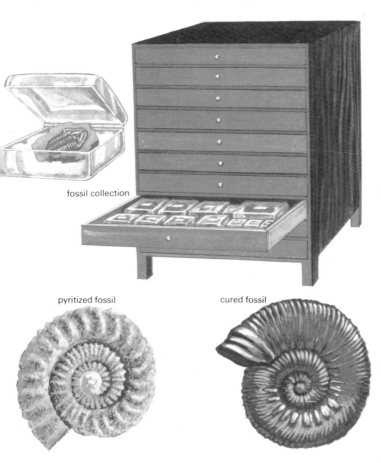

fossil collection

pyritized fossil

cured fossil

Fossils in decoration

The shape of many fossils is attractive in itself, and anyone not interested in the scientific aspects of palaeontology may still wish to collect them for this reason alone. The only barrier to their being used in much the same way as stones or pebbles is the fact that many of them are surprisingly fragile and cannot be handled so freely. In general, however, a fossil which is heavy for its size will stand up to a fair amount of use.

Large fossils are rarely come by, with the exception of size-able ammonites which are to be found in a number of Jurassic rock localities. These flat, spiral shells, which when alive housed creatures related to the present-day octopus, are often fantastically knurled and spined and make beautiful decorative objects in themselves. They can be put to some use as a doorstop, or even added as an interesting stone to a rock garden. Another find sometimes made in Jurassic rocks is the vertebra of an ichthyosaur. The shallowly biconcave discs have none of the complexity of shape of the vertebrae of land animals and a large one will make an interesting dish or ashtray.

For purely decorative purposes, the smaller fossil specimens are usually more suitable. Since prehistoric times fossils of many kinds have been used as amulets or other charms. One type found particularly often is the stem section of crinoids, or sea lilies, pierced to make a necklace. These small, geometrically shaped fragments may still be found in many places and could be used in this way today, although piercing could be replaced by modern adhesives and links bought from a shop that deals in do-it-yourself jewellery making.

Other fossils can be used to make such ornaments as bracelets, rings and earrings. If this is the aim of your collecting, you should look for specimens which match each other as closely as possible in size and shape or complement each other in some other way such as texture. You must beware of using specimens which might be pyritized, or your work will disintegrate as the fossils are eaten into by the acid. Bearing these considerations in mind, the beach will offer you a wide range of interesting and decorative objects in the form of fossils.

All sorts of decorative and useful objects may be made from fossils.

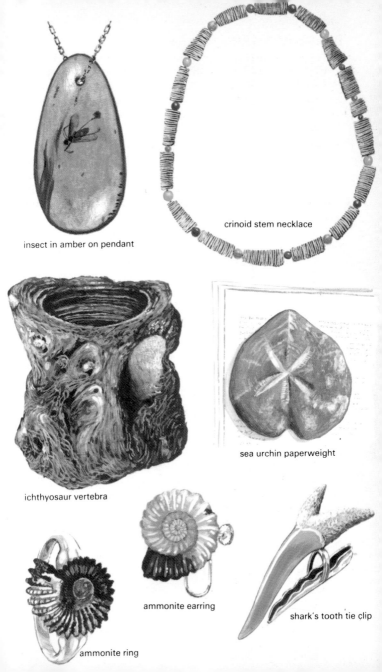

insect in amber on pendant

crinoid stem necklace

ichthyosaur vertebra

sea urchin paperweight

ammonite ring

ammonite earring

shark's tooth tie clip

PRESERVING SEAWEEDS

Piles of seaweed rotting on the beach are one of the less pleasant aspects of the seaside. Unattractive as they may be en masse, individually seaweeds are often very beautiful and the wave-wrenched piles of seaweed are worth exploring for some of the more delicate sublittoral species. Even the weeds to be found between the tides can make an interesting collection. They may be preserved in various ways, but the most usual method is to press them on to paper. To do this you should first wash the plant carefully in sea water, or tap water to which sea salt has been added, so that you can disentangle the complex fronds and clean away any grit. Large seaweeds can then be laid on a sheet of stiff paper, but the small, fine ones should be transferred to a shallow dish of salt water and the paper should be slid underneath the floating specimen.

The stages in pressing seaweeds.

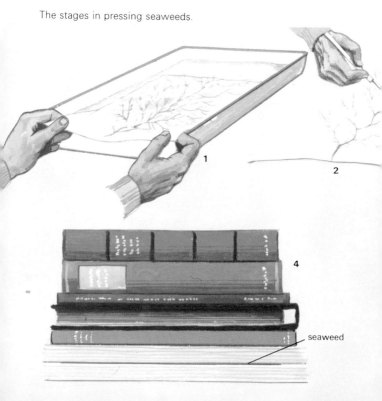

seaweed

The paper is then drawn out very gently with the plant in position on it. You will probably need to adjust it with a fine paintbrush or a mounted needle but when it is arranged to your liking, put the paper and specimen on to a piece of blotting paper. To protect your specimen cover it with a piece of muslin or fine cloth – pieces cut from old nylon tights serve this purpose very well – otherwise the seaweed will stick to the paper above as well as that below. Put plenty of blotting paper above and below the specimen and place it and the blotting paper into a plant press or under a pile of heavy books, and change the paper daily until the specimen is completely desiccated. You may then store it in a folder as part of a scientific collection, or with particularly beautiful specimens, such as the *Plocamium* in the illustration below, frame it as a decoration.

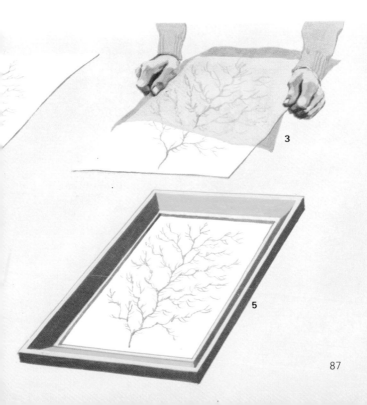

SHELLS

The shape of a shell is totally functional in the life of the animal that inhabits it. From a human viewpoint, however, the strengthening ribs or protective spines are often extremely beautiful, and because of this shells have been used in decoration since very early times. The shells sold in souvenir shops in seaside towns are generally tropical species, which were collected while the animals were still alive. Although a serious shell collector will take his specimens in this way, the beachcomber will be content with those that he can find empty and even on British shores one can pick up large whelk shells which can double as a decorative object and a small vase for single flowers.

Smaller shells are often extremely attractive, both in colour and surface texture. For example, the netted dog whelk is an abundant species which merits a second look and the wentletrap is well worth searching for near the lower tide mark. Even the commonest of sea snail shells may be transformed by the attentions of the sea which, when it breaks through the hard outer whorls of the shell, exposes the magically exact spiral of the columella around which the snail's body once curled. Random collections of small shells can be dust gatherers once you have taken them home and a simple way of dealing with them is to put them into a big sweet jar, filling it with the results of several years' holidays – the shapes and colours make a fascinating mosaic.

Apart from the shells of sea snails, those of bivalves or tusk shells may be picked up for their beauty or their curiosity value. Other sorts of shells may include those of sea urchins, which are often sold as decorations, but these are rarely found on the beach for they are fragile objects and are soon destroyed. The shells of crabs may also be found and these could play their part in decorative schemes, for they are quite robust and once dry are not unpleasant to handle. Be careful that it is a cast shell that you collect – if it is a dead crab, you will suffer from the powerful and unpleasant smell as it dries out.

The uses to which shells have been put are legion. Apart

Just a few of the many ornaments made by craftsmen, that have been inspired by the shapes of shells.

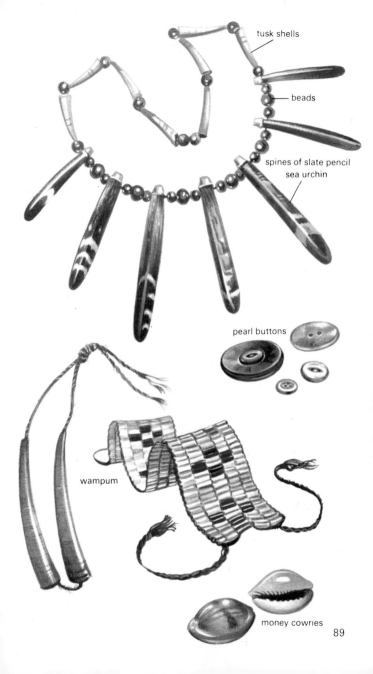

tusk shells

beads

spines of slate pencil
sea urchin

pearl buttons

wampum

money cowries

89

from being collected for their own sake – and collectors some-times pay large sums for particularly fine specimens – they have been used as money and for decoration (both personal and as inlays in furniture and other objects). Pearl buttons have been cut from shells, and skirts made of shells are worn in some Polynesian islands. They have also served as spoons, knives, and fishhooks. Once, tribes in the West Indies used the large conch shells as a substitute for stone to make axes large and strong enough to cut down trees.

Shells in decoration

The use of shells in decoration leads inevitably to putting several together in a more or less formal way to make objects which can at least be regarded as amusing knick-knacks and at a higher level as a minor form of art. The fluted shape of a limpet shell suggests a crinoline skirt, while the rounded body and pointed spire of a common periwinkle needs little trans-formation to become a mouse, with two tiny tellin shells as ears. The possibilities at this level are endless and the shapes of the different sorts of shells will suggest the different objects that you can make from them. If you want to try your hand at this, collect a lot of different shells from the beach, wash them in fresh water to get rid of the sand and salt and let them dry completely before you start work. Sort out the different kinds and sizes and use an impact adhesive, that sets hard, for stick-ing them together. Because many of the shells will be tiny – the mouse's ears, for example – it is better to handle them with a pair of fine tweezers, which will also help to prevent you from getting your fingers sticky.

A box decorated with shells also makes an attractive object. For this you will need a small wooden box, and you simply arrange and stick your shells over the top and sides. While you can do this in any way you please, you will soon find that you want to try making a formal pattern. This is more difficult and needs careful planning otherwise you may find that, having arranged your main pattern first, you are left with awkwardly shaped spaces which are difficult to fill. You need not limit yourself to using mollusc shells; small crab carapaces, part of an echinoderm shell or even the egg case of a whelk can make interesting additions to your pattern. When the box

Top A shell lady and a shell mouse are quickly and easily made. The frame for a favourite holiday photograph can be decorated with shells. *Above* Shells can be used to decorate boxes.

is finished, the shells can be varnished thinly to give them a wet-looking shine; it is not necessary, but many people feel that it improves the appearance of the work.

There are, of course, other natural objects from the shore

that may lend themselves to a decorative use. One that is worth experimenting with is cuttlebone, which can easily be carved in low relief. Before you start, wash the cuttlebone thoroughly in hot water and detergent and let it dry out. This will get rid of the fishy smell which otherwise lingers about it. Sketch your design on with a special pencil or ballpoint and cut away the parts you do not want. One side of the cuttlebone has a hard shell which is difficult to cut through; the other side is soft and can be worked easily, using the small blade of a penknife. The cuttlebone is formed as a series of layers and as you gain skill, you will find that you can use these as an integral part of your design.

So far we have been considering making fun objects which are relatively quick and easy to construct and which will cause little heartbreak if they are lost or broken. A more ambitious project, however, is the construction of a shell picture. A visit to almost any museum will show you examples of Victorian shell pictures, often exquisitely made, using thousands of tiny shells all neatly glued in place. The subjects vary from vases of flowers to pictorial representations of places and people. In some cases the shells may have been tinted, but in the best examples the natural colours speak for themselves. As with simpler designs, you will first need to make as large and varied a collection of shells as you possibly can and wash and sort them carefully before starting on your picture. A piece of stiff card is best for the base, but anything which will support the weight of the shells will do. Sketch the design on the board and stick the shells carefully in place, handling them with your tweezers and using a hard-drying glue. In the more complex shell pictures an interesting effect is often gained by overlapping large numbers of small venus or tellin shells, like the tiles on a roof, giving an almost level surface with an interesting, varied colour pattern. The picture is often completed with a frame of larger shells, such as dog whelk shells, necklace shells or small scallops which gives a sense of perspective to the whole.

Specially selected small shells which matched each other perfectly went into the making of this Victorian shell tray *(top)*, and into the design below, based on a nineteenth century whaler's valentine.

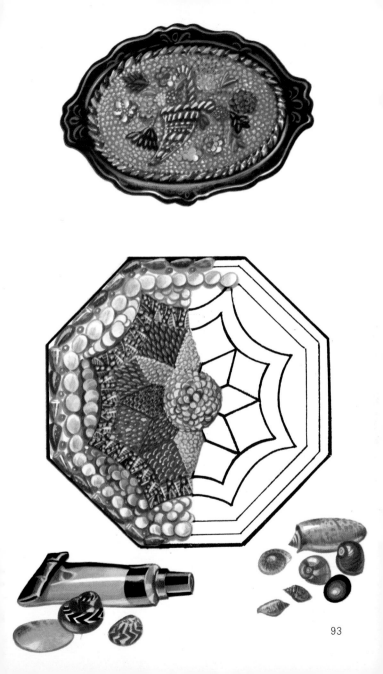

The beauty of shells has led to their widespread use in jewellery, their most valuable product being the pearls which are made by bivalve molluscs. Precious pearls are obtained from various species of oyster, which live below the tide line, but mussels on the beach often contain tiny, commercially valueless pearls. Mother-of-pearl may also be used, either in inlay work or to make medallions cut from some of the heavier species.

Although it may be beautiful to look at, the type of jewellery made with shells is usually of the semiprecious kind. If you want to make a bracelet or necklace of shells, for example, as with other craft work you will need to collect more than your original estimate for the job, for there are almost bound to be some too fragile to use or unsuitable for some other reason. Cowries are favourites for this sort of work; there are two British species, similar in length and general appearance. They need careful searching for, but are present on most beaches in the south and west, although you may have to look for a long time before you have enough for your purpose. One way of making them secure is by drilling a tiny hole at either

Haliotis shells provide the decorative, brightly coloured mother-of-pearl used both in modern jewellery, and in antique pieces.

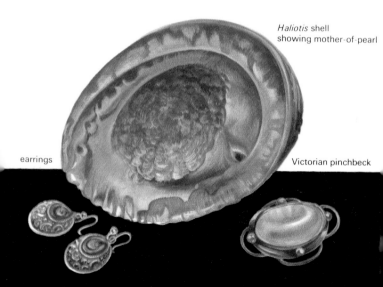

Haliotis shell
showing mother-of-pearl

earrings

Victorian pinchbeck

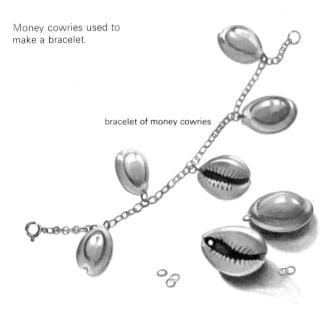

Money cowries used to make a bracelet.

bracelet of money cowries

end, and then threading them on a fine nylon cord perhaps using other small shells as spacers but, as with pebble jewellery, you can use linked metal mounts on which the shells may be stuck. The final effect will be very pleasing in either case.

When shell hunting on a sandy beach you may often find a bivalve which has been neatly bored through with a tiny hole about one millimetre in diameter. This is the work of the necklace shell, and it is possible to use its efforts in your work.

A type of shell very popular with jewellery-makers is called *Haliotis*. This has a wonderfully coloured, iridescent inner layer, and the usual method of using it is to saw the shell into the shapes required and mount the medallions on to metal attachments to make earrings, brooches, necklaces, etc. *Haliotis* occurs in warm, coastal waters throughout the world, although in Britain it is present only in the Channel Islands where it is known as the ormer. Because it is also good to eat, it is becoming rare in many places due to over-collecting. In some areas it is now a protected species, but pieces of *Haliotis* can often still be bought for use in shell work.

Elaborate shell jewellery

A visit to almost any jeweller who specializes in antique pieces is sure to show you examples of elaborate decorations in which shells have been used. Sometimes small shells are mounted with semiprecious stones, as in one particular kind of bracelet which uses shells found in the Persian Gulf set with turquoises and silver. Complex necklaces in which huge numbers of tiny shells were strung together were often made by tropical islanders and may sometimes be found in curio shops, although the workmanship on these articles can be very crude. A more refined form of shell work is seen in the cameo, which is cut from the heavy armour of warm water helmet shells. In these animals the shells have layers of different colours which are utilized in the design. This is usually a portrait or a classical motif which shows as a pale subject on a dark background and is generally mounted to make a brooch or a ring, although any function for which a medallion can be used is suitable. Most cameos are cut in Italy, and the craft is one beyond the average amateur for the shells are extremely hard and difficult to work.

Shells of many kinds have inspired craftsmen of the past. The example of a shore crab's carapace cast in gold is a simple instance of an effective ornament being based on the gleanings of the beach. Other, more complex works may involve the embellishment of a shell (either real or fashioned from precious metal) with gems of various kinds. Examples of this may be seen in many museums and art galleries. In other artefacts the shell is merely the starting point of the design which, like the commonplace Victorian spoon warmer, takes the shell form but is changed as the artist thinks fit, for the functional purpose that he has in mind.

Goldsmithing and silversmithing is taught at many art schools and although the beginner might have to curtail his ambitions for a while, the use of seashore objects either for inspiration or themselves decorated in various ways, perhaps even with polished pebbles, should be borne in mind as a fruitful source of basic material for work. Whatever your shell work involves, from the simplest glueing together of common limpet and whelk shells to the refinements of treating them like gems, it should give pleasure both in the making and the beholding.

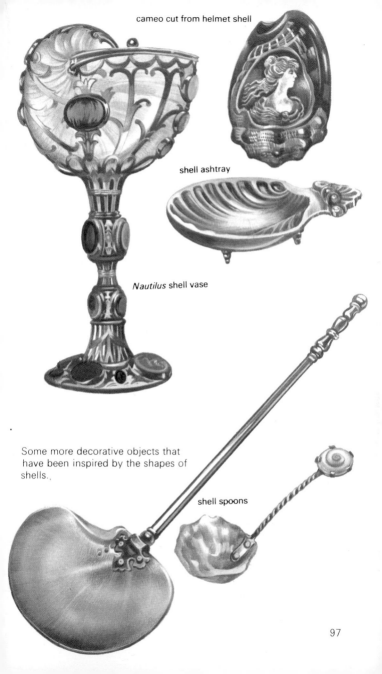

cameo cut from helmet shell

shell ashtray

Nautilus shell vase

Some more decorative objects that have been inspired by the shapes of shells.

shell spoons

PLASTIC EMBEDDING

In making jewellery from fossils and shells it is necessary to use objects which have a degree of robustness not shared by everything that you might find on the beach. A way of overcoming this is to use the technique of embedding the find in clear plastic. This makes it possible for a delicate find, which would otherwise have to be kept untouched in a box or cupboard, to be seen and handled freely.

Plastic embedding kits can be bought quite cheaply and include a quantity of liquid plastic and a hardener which must be added to make it set. Because the quantities used are quite critical, there is usually a small measuring cylinder as well as trays of different shapes in which to make the cast. Full instructions are provided and these must be followed carefully to obtain the best results.

The illustration shows the steps in embedding an Aristotle's lantern, which is the mouthparts and teeth of a sea urchin. It is a difficult object to embed and it might be better to try your hand at first with something smaller and less likely to contain air bubbles. The following hints are worth remembering: 1. Once the plastic has set it cannot be removed from most surfaces, so prepare a good working space somewhere that you can be reasonably sure won't be disturbed by small children or animals. 2. The plastic has a rather unpleasant smell, so your working place should be well ventilated. 3. You will need to make up a small amount of plastic to line the mould, before mixing the full amount. Instructions do not always make this clear. 4. The plastic and hardener should be mixed very thoroughly, but very slowly, or air bubbles will form. 5. The plastic, when mixed, should be poured very slowly on to the object, again to prevent air bubbles. 6. It is possible to get rid of air bubbles by moving the object slightly in the plastic, but be careful not to upset the design or symmetry of an arrangement. 7. When the plastic has hardened, the upper surface will need to be polished. The sooner this is done the better, so make sure that you have the right grades of wet and dry emery paper handy before you start.

Stages in embedding an Aristotle's lantern.

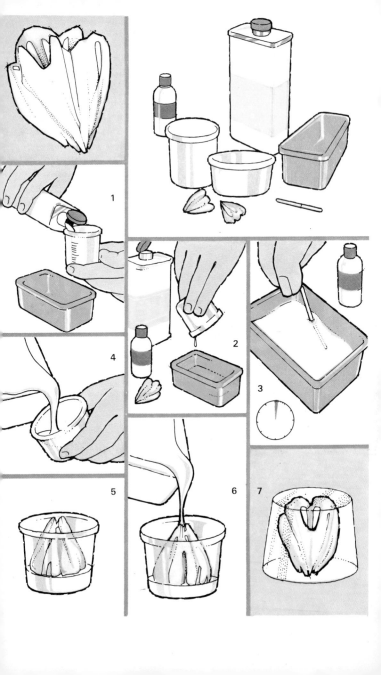

TREASURE HUNTING

Almost everybody dreams of finding buried treasure at some time, with gold doubloons spilling from the mouldering chest in which they have been hidden. The seaside is sometimes the scene of just such discoveries now that modern diving methods have made it possible to explore some of the ancient ships which foundered long ago on offshore rocks. In a very few cases such ships may be explored briefly at low tide, but they are not the province of the average beach treasure hunter who must restrict himself to more mundane discoveries. As we have seen, the beach can yield many natural treasures but it may also be the source of other man-made objects, some at least of which may have an intrinsic value.

In searching for shells, pebbles or fossils, the beachcomber generally wishes to visit the shores which are least frequented by other people. When looking for valuables on the beach, he will want to go to the places which are busiest at the peak holiday times of the year. The articles that he may find include spectacles, watches, pens, cameras, rings and other jewellery and, most likely of all, coins. It must be remembered that of all these, coins are the only objects which may be kept with impunity. The thrill of finding, say, a ring, must be tempered by the thought that it must be handed over to the proper authority as soon as possible. Its fate depends on a number of circumstances: in some cases, if it is not claimed it may become yours; in others, it may be sold and part of the proceeds become

Holiday crowds often leave 'souvenirs' of their presence behind them.

yours; even if it is claimed, you may benefit by a reward. Not to report such a discovery could conceivably lead to a charge of stealing by finding.

If you want to search for lost coins and other valuables, it is obvious that the best time will be when the crowds have disappeared. If you are coin hunting the best time is in the evening or early morning when you can walk along with the sun low in the sky, so that you can see the enlarged shadows of any small object in the sand. Once you have got your eye in, coins will spring to your notice. If you are hunting after high tide has smoothed the sand, it is worth looking well up on the beach for the coins will act as pebbles and may be carried above the place where they were dropped. Although you may make a lucky find with an inspired and imaginative swoop, it is better to quarter the beach carefully, scanning each line as you walk along your chosen pitch. You may feel that holiday beachcombing should be fun, and should not involve hard concentration, but it can be worthwhile. Some people make a regular practice of beachcombing for money, furrowing the sand with a short stick to enable them to examine a larger area more thoroughly. They go down to the shore early in the day, whenever the tide is low, throughout the holiday season. In a good week they may discover many coins, almost all of small value but totalling a value of several pounds.

The experienced coin hunter on the beach will probably not rely on his eyes alone to find his trophies but will most

likely turn the surface of the sand, either with a small rake or a stick, making a furrow across the most likely places. This is certainly a way to increase your chance of finding coins but in recent years a new piece of equipment, which greatly improves the likelihood of a find, has become available. This is the metal detector, which will indicate the presence of metal even though it might be buried several centimetres below the surface.

Metal detectors are small, lightweight pieces of electronic equipment which involve the use of at least one tuned circuit, the balance of which will be upset by the near presence of metal, particularly iron, although all metals will cause it to react to some extent. In appearance the detector usually looks rather like a small cigar box on the end of a walking stick and, in use, the box is passed with slow, sweeping movements over the surface of the sand. Its method of informing you of the presence of metal depends on the design: there may be a meter to record the interference, or it may rely on an audible signal. If you use a detector under dry conditions, the results tend to be better; on the beach the dampness of the sand tends to reduce its efficiency, but it can, in effect, see below the immediate surface for you. If you decide to use one, remember that the machine cannot distinguish between a piece of driftwood with a nail stuck in it and a really valuable discovery, and you will certainly find more nails, bolts and shackles than coins or rings. Even if you only succeed in discovering fairly modest treasures, you will probably enjoy beachcombing in this way. If you decide that you want to use a metal detector you can obtain one at a fairly modest price from dealers in electronic goods, or you may like to try your hand at building one. Kits are also available from some firms to enable you to do this.

It is illegal to use a metal detector in Britain without a pipe-finder licence which can be obtained from the Home Office (Radio Regulatory Division). You should also check to make sure there is no local council opposition to the use of metal detectors on your chosen site.

The traditional *(right)* and the modern way of searching for beach treasure.

GLASS AND BOTTLES

The fact that glass is brittle and shatters easily into sharp fragments makes it one of the hazards of the beach. The action of
the sea is not always one of strong pounding, however. Lesser
abrasion with sand often reduces pieces of glass from their
original razor-edged condition to a smooth, flat shape – a
similar effect to that exerted on beach pebbles. Some of the
prettiest objects to be found on the beach are pieces of old
bottle glass, especially blue, green or amber colours, worn
down to irregular but smooth shapes. A collection in a jar
makes an attractive ornament, or a mosaic of pieces can be
glued to the outside of an inkpot to make an unusual candle-
holder.

One of the most sought-after glass objects which may be
found intact on the beach is an old-fashioned net float. Large
numbers of these coloured balls were used on the upper edges
of seine nets, but have been largely replaced today by less
fragile plastic floats. The most likely place to look for a glass
float is on a really remote beach, where it may have become
wedged between rocks and so have gone unnoticed by other
visitors. It is likely that in the future they may be regarded as
quite valuable collector's items, for the floats which can be
bought in tourist souvenir shops these days are made for that
purpose and are far less robust than the original article.

The fact that a hollow, glass vessel will float means that
bottles are among the commonest finds in the beach debris,
often having been brought a considerable distance by wind,
tides and currents. The storybook situation of shipwrecked
mariners appealing for help by launching a bottle containing
a message is not entirely imaginary although if a bottle containing such a message were found on a British beach, children
are most likely to have been responsible. Another sort of
message may be found in drift bottles, which are released in
large numbers as part of research programmes into the direction
and speed of ocean currents. These bottles are designed to
float, or to be carried in mid-water, or in some cases to bounce

Glass net floats and drift bottles are rare but possible finds on some
beaches. More common are screw-type bottles with messages from
holiday-makers.

Old-fashioned stone or glass ginger beer bottles can still be found intact on some remote beaches. Milk bottles and plastic bottles are unfortunately only too common.

along the seabed. Inside they carry an addressed card which should be returned to the research station which initiated the work. In general, a small reward is offered for the return of the card filled in with the details of the place where the bottle made a landfall. This may appear to be a crude method of discovering the direction of tides and currents, but by duplicating the journey taken by fish eggs, the places where the fry hatch and begin their larval life are discovered. In some cases heavy plastic envelopes containing a similar card have been used and plastic mushrooms called 'woodhead drifters' are yet other devices for recording information about ocean currents.

Other bottles which occur on the beach include those made to hold wine, beer or ginger beer. Usually they have long since lost their labels, but they may be quite interesting shapes and colours. Much rarer and more exciting to find are the old-fashioned ginger beer bottles with a pointed end. Some of these were sealed with a glass marble in the neck, but it is unusual to find them intact for the boys who drank the pop would break the neck of the bottle to extract the marble. Nevertheless the rarity of the find increases its excitement and value. Stone ginger beer bottles with their embossed legend also make interesting finds, although the most interesting of all – a wrecked cargo of full bottles – is very rare indeed. There are stories dating back to the Second World War of ships carrying cargoes of spirits wrecked within reach of the shores of some of the western islands of Britain. The situations which followed were reminiscent of that dramatized by Compton Mackenzie in *Whisky Galore.*

Today, glass bottles on the beach are accompanied and out-numbered by plastic containers. Unsinkable, unbreakable, and to all intents and purposes indestructible, these now make up a major part of the strandline litter. As the use of plastics increases, so does the mountain of waste jettisoned into the sea by the increasing number of small boat sailors, adding to the bobbing army which eventually ends up on the coastline. The plastic cups thrown from cross-channel ferry services used to be among the most obtrusive waste to be found on the south coast of England. Now that there has been a move to retain them for proper dispersal on land their numbers will diminish, although there are enough plastic containers in the sea to dis-figure the beaches for many years to come. The development of a properly biodegradable plastic must be something which every seaside visitor hopes for, for it would reduce the un-lovely and useless litter on so many beaches.

Fragments of broken glass can be used to make attractive ornaments.

Masses of vegetation are often swept out to sea by tropical floods.

DRIFTWOOD

Man has for generations regarded the sea as the biggest dust-bin in the world and has tipped waste and rubbish of all kinds into it, confident that it would finally disappear if only to land on his neighbour's beach. Most of the natural waste from the land also ends in the oceans, usually carried there by the rivers which run into the sea with their cargo of silt and other debris. Rivers in spate may carry many things, but dead wood forms a large part of their burden. This often takes the form of great rafts of vegetation, which may survive intact for months whilst being swung slowly round the oceans on the major currents. In temperate rivers which are used for navigation such a mass of timber would be broken up because it would constitute a hazard to shipping, but many tropical rivers carry huge quantities of wood to the sea each year, mainly trees torn from the river banks in times of flood.

Gradually the wood becomes waterlogged, bored by ship-worms, and plays host to goose barnacles and other encrusting

108

organisms. Much is eventually destroyed but some survives to be cast up as driftwood on a shore, perhaps thousands of kilometres from its country of origin. Some plants use the movements of the sea to carry their seeds. Coconuts are perhaps the best known, but these can travel for short distances only before becoming waterlogged and thus unable to grow when they finally reach land. They cannot hope to do more than colonize neighbouring islands. Any long-distance hops between islands must have been made with human help and indeed man has carried the coconut palm with him throughout the tropics.

Mangrove fruit fare better; they can survive long sea journeys without harm and there is no doubt that the mangroves on many remote islands have arrived there by natural means. The seeds of some large beans also make long sea journeys. Two species, protected by their heavy outer coats, sometimes survive the trip from the West Indies to the south-west coasts of Britain, brought here on the flow of the Gulf Stream and the North Atlantic Drift. They are not common, nor are they still able to germinate, but they are found sufficiently frequently and are still hard enough to be the traditional

Coconuts, seeds of tropical beans and mangrove pods may be swept long distances by sea currents.

mangrove pods

coconut

tropical beans

object given to babies in parts of south Wales to help them with their teething.

Although the trunks and gnarled branches among the wood on a beach proclaim their origin as natural drift, much reaches the sea as part of lost cargoes or broken objects of various kinds which can always be distinguished from natural driftwood as it will be cut or fashioned in some way. Sometimes the hull of a boat may be found rotting on a beach. This is less likely to be a shipwrecked hulk than the remains of a boat which has become unseaworthy and so left to end her days on the shore. Anything useful would almost certainly have been stripped from such a craft, however.

Many of the floating planks in the sea come from deck cargoes of timber which have been washed overboard in heavy weather between Scandinavia and Britain, which imports soft woods from northern Europe for use in building. Some of these cargoes get carried to the islands of the far north, where they accumulate on remote beaches, but those which fetch up in more populated places are usually removed promptly by beachcombers who can find many uses for them, and who sometimes spirit away huge baulks of timber which look as though they should defy removal. Raw timber is, however, only part of the driftwood that is lost from ships and often the

Cargo ships often lose part of their freight in heavy seas.

Broken crates and parts of cargoes washed ashore after a storm.

beaches to which the flotsam of the sea is swept have an astonishing assortment of wooden objects. Hatch covers seem to be lost with great regularity. They are usually strongly made and so are found intact, although in future there may be fewer of them as the fashion for steel hatch covers is growing and these sink irrevocably once they are lost. Spars and oars often survive intact but crates, which figure largely in the debris, are often smashed so that only individual planks can be salvaged from them.

Occasionally unexpected articles turn up – benches or chairs, miraculously undamaged, or a fragment of carving, which was once part of a picture frame, its gilt only slightly worn. The state of the wood can give an indication as to the length of its journey. Timber which has been floating for a long time in inshore waters is often contaminated with oil and while planks which have been swept across the open sea may have encountered an oil slick, they are more likely to show signs of the length of their voyage by the growth of sea creatures which have settled on them. On a long journey shipworms may have completely honeycombed the once firm wood, and goose barnacles may adorn it so thickly that there seems to be no room for any further occupants.

A coastal cottage with its store of beachcombed objects waiting to be put to good use.

Uses for driftwood

There are not many people who can claim – like the inhabitant of one remote northern island – that every stick of furniture in his house came from the beach, but certainly driftwood can be put to many uses. The most obvious is as fuel and the beachcomber can be assured of a stock of wood for burning through even the longest winter. Drying it out is often less of a problem than might be expected, but your woodpile should have good ventilation and some cover. Once dry, the wood will burn as well as any other although the salt which has been left in it may produce flames of interesting colours.

Fencing is another use to which driftwood can be put. It is rare to find palings or fence boards but pit props can make excellent fence posts to which wire or, as may be seen round some seaside cottages, an assortment of boards rescued from the sea may be attached. Garden furniture, benches and the like can often be assembled easily enough from clean driftwood; indoor fittings are more difficult to come by, but with luck and some ingenuity a determined beachcomber can achieve much in time.

The average holiday-maker, however, will not wish to burden himself with quantities of timber for burning or fencing. His search for wood will more likely be confined to the natural drift, especially the roots, which are often twisted and gnarled into fantastic shapes. These objets trouvés sometimes appear to bear a resemblance to other objects and a holiday art gallery of appropriately named pieces can provide a lot of family fun. You may feel that the water-polished shapes merit more than a holiday game and join the many people who take pieces of drift home to use as ornaments or holiday mementos. In some cases the work of the sea cannot be improved on, but you may wish to accentuate the strange shape that you have found either by carving or sandpapering to smooth some of the curves still further. You may even wish to cut small pieces for use as pendants or as parts of rings or earrings. These will need to be selected carefully, then sandpapered and mounted as you think appropriate. For a pendant, a leather bootlace threaded through a natural hole may be sufficient; for other jewellery similar mounts as for pebble jewellery will be best.

Driftwood may be used to make interesting shapes, and small pieces can be polished and used as pendants.

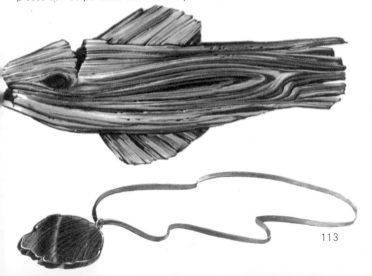

FLOTSAM AND JETSAM

One of the delights of beachcombing is the element of the unexpected which is always present. This is never more so than when one finds objects lost from boats, although these may sometimes remind us that in the west country of Britain, beachcombing is known as wrecking. The sinister reputation of the inhabitants of the cliffed western coasts of Britain, who during the last century were said to have used false lights to lure ships on to rocks so that they could benefit from the wreck, is undeserved. Nevertheless their part of the world is one of the best for beachcombers, with all sorts of booty to be found on the shore, while the collection of figureheads to be seen on Tresco, in the Isles of Scilly, is a reminder that many ships have in fact foundered in these dangerous seas.

On board a ship, anything not securely lashed down is likely to be swept from over the side in times of storm and may find itself among the flotsam of the beach. The dinghies often towed by small seagoing boats are a case in point. Although towing may save valuable deck room, it is a procedure which can easily result in the loss of the dinghy if the wind or sea rises. Since such small craft are usually highly buoyant, they will ride like corks until they finally drift ashore. Even if the dinghy is brought aboard the oars may be lost if they are not properly secured and the same applies to fenders, whether they are merely old car tyres or smartly made ones of plaited fibre. The paravane self-steering equipment of small ocean-going boats is also vulnerable and parts of this may sometimes be found ashore, although it is very unlikely to remain undamaged.

By their very nature lifebuoys and liferafts float and if lost may eventually be washed ashore. If a name is discernible on them the coastguards should be informed at once, for although it is most likely that the lifebuoy was lost in normal circumstances, it may be evidence of a missing vessel. If the name is obliterated there is nothing you can do, although you may find the cork of which they are made useful in a number of ways, including making bases for some of your

Parts of boats may often be washed ashore after storms.

Buoys which have come adrift usually end up on the shore. They should be reported to the coastguard if found.

beach finds which might otherwise scratch the furniture or shelf where you intend to keep them.

Ropes may also find their way ashore, although the neat coil on deck is liable to have been unravelled by the waves and stiffened by salt and sand. If you intend to make use of your find, it is as well to know what sort of line you have for they do not all have the same properties. Unfortunately ropes of natural fibres (nylon and terylene), which would be very useful, are heavy and tend to sink and are rarely found. Polythene and polypropylene ropes float and may be beached in knotted bundles, but they are of dubious value for they may have deteriorated without giving any indication.

Netting of various sorts is fairly common but usually in quantities too small to be of any use, other perhaps than in a garden supporting climbing plants. Sailcloth is rare in pieces of a usable size, but buckets, which are occasionally lost from boats, may float ashore and can immediately be useful to augment the haversack and polythene bags which any beach-comber will have with him to carry home his beach gleanings. These can include fruit – especially oranges and grapefruit – which is often found, and which can survive undamaged after several days in the sea. Fruit, together with electric light bulbs which always seem to be present on the shore, may be part of a lost deck cargo, or part of the rubbish which is tipped overboard by every seagoing boat. Most of this offal mercifully sinks, or is eaten by sea birds or fishes, but the large numbers of flip-flop sandals as well as other shoes and pieces of clothing, are just as likely to have been lost by land-based holiday-makers as by sailors.

A much more important find would be a buoy. Navigational buoys are not likely to be lost for they are large and well maintained with frequent inspection, but the small buoys which are used to mark the position of lobster pots or set fishing lines do sometimes come adrift, and float in to the shore. These buoys, which are called dan-buoys, normally carry a coloured flag to make them easier to see. They may be home-made, but most are made of inflated plastic which is very tough. The buoy should carry the registration number of the vessel to which it belongs and anybody finding one should hand it as soon as possible to the Receiver of Wreck who will contact the owner, for unmarked fishing gear represents a serious danger to inshore shipping.

Cork is easily carved and can be turned to a variety of uses.

BEACH HAZARDS

Natural dangers

A fact which beachcombing will quickly bring home to anyone is the power of the sea. The sight of a log which rested lightly on the waves and was then thrown well above the line of the normal high tide in a storm, proving too heavy for a man to shift, together with the rattling gravel in the undertow, are both reminders that the beach can be a dangerous place. Anybody intending to spend any time there should remember this and take reasonable precautions against the inherent dangers.

The first precaution is to ascertain the times of the tides. It is dangerous as well as frightening to be cut off by high water, so remember not to explore small coves which can be reached only at dead-low water unless you are sure that there is another way out. The turning tide can bring currents swirling back round the point and your retreat can quickly become impassable. Secondly, remember that sea cliffs are on the whole

Always pay attention to warning signs on beaches. This one warns of crumbling cliffs.

A cross section through the sand showing how the weever fish lies with only its poisonous spines projecting.

more dangerous than inland crags, for wind and water work at them incessantly to loosen fragments. It is as well not to walk too close to the foot of the cliff and if you are collecting fossils beware of the danger of falling rock. Never neglect signs warning of danger from this, or from quicksands which form if waterlogged fine sand overlies gravel or a coarse substrate of some sort. Take no chances for there are places, even round the coasts of Britain, where you could be engulfed entirely.

Another danger of the sandy shore is the weever fish which gets its name from an ancient word for a viper. This gives a clue to the danger it presents for it carries poison glands behind its head and a long, sharp, grooved spine, by which the poison can be introduced into a wound which will be made in anyone who treads on the fish. This is more likely than it might seem, for the weever fish remains on the beach at low tide – almost completely buried in the sand – in places where shallow pools have been left behind by the retreating water. The damage done by the weever is unlikely to be fatal but it is extremely painful, and anybody hurt in this way would certainly have to spend a day resting, and the foot could well be sore for a week or more. Fishermen who have sometimes caught and handled a weever accidentally, say that the pain will not go until the tide has fallen twice. The only way to be sure of not being harmed by weevers is to wear shoes when on the beach, a rule which must be adhered to if you are fossicking on tropical shores where a number of poisonous organisms may occur.

Man-made dangers

It is not only natural dangers which can beset the beach-comber, for man also adds many hazards to the environment. The glass bottle thrown into the sea, or left on the beach, may get broken and until the water and sand have dulled the sharp edges, can be a major danger to bare feet. An even more common hazard is oil, which may be spilt into the sea as the result of an accident, or forms as a slick because an oil tanker has been washing out its tanks at sea – a practice which is now forbidden by the major oil companies. In either case, sticky, evil-smelling, black, tarry oil may come ashore fouling the beaches, killing large numbers of animals and making it impossible for holiday-makers or beachcombers

The Portuguese man o' war is a natural hazard occurring most frequently on beaches in the warmer parts of the world; the others shown here are all man made.

to enjoy themselves. It is difficult to remove from oneself, or from shoes, clothing or towels, which may be damaged beyond cleaning. The only way to combat this menace is to join the conservation bodies which pressure the government and oil companies to outlaw careless handling of the oil.

Other lost cargoes may be more directly dangerous. Many lethal chemicals are used in industry and agriculture and containers of such substances are sometimes lost from ships. Usually this is reported and police and coastguards are alerted but anybody finding a drum of, say, insecticide should tell the police or coastguard immediately. Other hazards which still occur round the coasts are hangovers from the Second World War, when certain sea areas were mined and beaches defended with wire and explosives. Most of these were removed at the end of hostilities but a few escaped detection. Even today, mines and other explosive devices are swept ashore. Never consider that such an object or any part of it could be useful or taken as a souvenir – report your discovery to the authorities immediately.

BEACH LAW

The law relating to the beach and anything on it is, in general, obscure, for while the foreshore of most of the coastline of Britain belongs to the Crown and the public has access to it, there are many exceptions. So far as the average holiday-maker is concerned, the law and its vagaries need not bother him. If you wish to collect seaweed for laver bread, or shrimps, winkles or mussels for a meal, nobody will prevent you, although if an exceptionally low tide uncovers an oyster bed you must desist, for these molluscs are farmed under licence.

If you wish to try your luck beachcombing for coins or other valuables, you may begin to find yourself in the maze of regulations which govern the ownership of man-made objects on the beach. Technically, everything belongs to someone and while there is much in the strandline that nobody wants, it is an offence to take something of value. If you find something such as a diamond ring, your best procedure is to take it to the police.

If you find something which has been lost at sea, it should be reported to the Receiver of Wreck who is usually the local customs officer and who has remarkably wide powers regarding lost cargoes, the prevention of looting of wrecked craft and the recovery of objects removed from the beach. Although he would not welcome packing cases or oranges, anything of value must be reported to him. You may still ultimately benefit from the sale of your find by receiving a reward.

Another official that you might need to contact is the coastguard who, as his name suggests, keeps a watch on what is going on around the shore. Shipping is logged and information regarding it is passed from one station to the next as a safeguard, especially in times of bad weather. Coastguards will probably be the first to notice a ship in distress, or an oil slick approaching the beach, but anything out of the ordinary on the shore should be reported to them. They have intimate knowledge of the tides and currents in their area, and they make weather observations which help to build up our understanding of the continuously changing picture of the shore.

If you see a distress flare fired from a ship, report it at once to the police or coastguard.

BOOKS TO READ

British Bivalve Seashells by N. Tebble. British Museum (Natural History), London, 1967.

British Caenozoic Fossils (1971), *British Mesozoic Fossils* (1972), *British Palaeozoic Fossils* (1969). British Museum (Natural History), London.

British Turtles by C. D. Brongersma. British Museum (Natural History), London, 1967.

Collins Pocket Guide to the Sea Shore by J. H. Barrett and C. M. Yonge. Collins, London, 1958.

Food for Free by R. Mabey. Collins, London, 1972.

Pebble Polishing and Pebble Jewellery by C. Rogers. Hamlyn, London, 1973.

The Pebbles on the Beach by C. Ellis. Faber, London, 1965.

The Sea Coast by J. A. Steers. Collins, London, 1953.

PLACES TO VISIT

Seaside museums often have interesting displays, as well as valuable information on local conditions. The Natural History Museum in London, the Royal Scottish Museum in Edinburgh and the National Museum of Wales in Cardiff all have large collections of natural objects which have been found on the beach.

INTERESTING BEACHES

In general, rocky coastlines are found in the north and west of Britain and along the coast of Brittany. Gower Bay and Harlech Bay in Wales, the north Lancashire coast, the coast of Fifeshire and part of the Norfolk coast all have large stretches of sand. In Europe, much of the coastline of Germany and the long coast of the Landes region in France also have long, sandy beaches. Mochras, or Shell Island, at the southern end of Harlech Bay is famous for the enormous number of shells that are swept there by the sea. Many fine pebbles can be collected on beaches in the north and west of Britain.

INDEX

Page numbers in **bold** type refer to illustrations